BEST RADIO
PLAYS OF 1986

BEST RADIO PLAYS OF 1986

The Giles Cooper Award Winners

Robert Ferguson: Dreams, Secrets, Beautiful Lies
Christina Reid: The Last of a Dyin' Race
Andrew Rissik: A Man Alone: Anthony
Ken Whitmore: The Gingerbread House
Valerie Windsor: Myths and Legacies

METHUEN/BBC PUBLICATIONS

First published in Great Britain in 1987 by Methuen London Ltd,
11 New Fetter Lane, London EC4P 4EE and in the United States of
America by Methuen Inc, 29 West 35th Street, New York NY 10001,
and BBC ... lone, 55 Marylebone High Street, London W1M 4AA.

Phototypeset in 9pt Garamond by
Words & Pictures Ltd, Thornton Heath, Surrey

Printed and bound in Great Britain
by Biddles Ltd,
Guildford and King's Lynn

British Library Cataloguing in Publication Data

Best radio plays of 1986: the Giles Cooper
    Award Winners.
    1. Radio plays, English
822'.02'08   PR1259.R33

ISBN 0-413-15770-9

CAUTION
These plays are fully protected by copyright. Any enquiries
concerning the rights for professional or amateur stage production,
broadcasting, readings etc., should be made to the authors'
respective agents, as follows:
Robert Ferguson: Michael Imison Playwrights Ltd, 28 Almeida Street,
London N1
Christina Reid: Goodwin Associates, 12 Rabbit Row, Kensington
Church Street, London W8 4DX
Andrew Rissik: Margaret Ramsay Ltd, 14a Goodwin's Court,
St Martin's Lane, London WC2N 4LL
Ken Whitmore: Harvey Unna & Stephen Durbridge,
24 Pottery Lane, Holland Park, London W11 4LZ
Valerie Windsor: MBA Literary Agents Ltd, 45 Fitzroy Street,
London W1P 5HR

CONTENTS

THE GILES COOPER AWARDS: a note on the selection

Giles Cooper

As one of the most original and inventive radio playwrights of the post-war years, Giles Cooper was the author who came most clearly to mind when the BBC and Methuen were in search of a name when first setting up their jointly sponsored radio drama awards in 1978. Particularly so, as the aim of the awards is precisely to encourage original radio writing by both new and established authors – encouragement in the form of both public acclaim and of publication of their work in book form.

Eligibility

Eligible for the awards was every original radio play first broadcast by the BBC domestic service from December 1985 to December 1986 (almost 500 plays in total). Excluded from consideration were translations, adaptations and dramatised 'features'. In order to ensure that the broad range of radio playwriting was represented, the judges aimed to select plays which offered a variety of length, subject matter and technique by authors with differing experience of writing for radio.

Selection

The editors-in-charge and producers of the various drama 'slots' were each asked to put forward about five or six plays for the judges' consideration. This resulted in a 'short-list' of some 30 plays from which the final selection was made. The judges were entitled to nominate further plays for consideration provided they were eligible. Selection was made on the strength of the script rather than of the production, since it was felt that the awards were primarily for writing and that production could unduly enhance or detract from the merits of the original script.

Judges

The judges for the 1986 awards were:
  Robert Cushman, freelance writer, formerly the *Observer* drama critic
  Nicholas Hern, Drama Editor, Methuen London
  Richard Imison, Deputy Head of BBC Radio Drama
  B.A. Young, who was formerly the *Financial Times* drama critic, and who now
    writes on radio for the same paper

PREFACE

The Old Hearplay

In the autumn of 1985, a distinguished group of writers, composers and producers from all round the world met together in the ancient city of Cologne to discuss modern concepts of creative radio. The 'Acustica International', as the gathering was called, was hosted by the German station Westdeutscher Rundfunk and its theme was 'Composers as *Hörspiel*-makers'. It was inventive and ambitious and involved several days of discussion, demonstration and public performance which led one of its organisers, Klaus Schöning of WDR's drama department, to surmise that the *Hörspiel* as a manifestation of creative radio had effectively been redefined. Yet I think it would not be unfair to say that its impact on the professional makers of radio drama and features in Great Britain – not to mention the millions in this country who listen to such things when they are broadcast – was minimal.

Which is a shame. Because the definition of the *Hörspiel* is at the heart of any discussion of radio drama as an art form, and the fact that the English language has – in England at any rate – no equivalent term, has done much to create public and professional confusion about what a radio play actually is.

Hörspiel means literally 'Hearplay' or perhaps 'hearing- or listening-play', which is straightforward enough although the German word *spiel* has, in addition to the double meanings of 'play' in English, the useful extra one of 'game'. Traditionally, it has been used in Germany to denote radio drama in a conventional narrative sense, so that *Hörspiel* and 'Radio Play' could for many years have been taken to describe the same thing – whatever that happened to be.

But there was, I think, a distinct advantage to be gained from a term that was not derived from the stage and therefore continually reminded the listener that whatever similarities might be found between a play on radio and a play in the theatre, they were essentially different experiences. (It says more about the historical structure of the BBC than the nature of radio drama as an art form that so many long-standing series titles end in the word 'Theatre' – or did, until recent determined efforts to replace most of them with the word 'Play'.)

It *may* have been due to this important difference of nomenclature, or perhaps to other factors of national temperament or institutional structure, that from the earliest days of broadcasting some people in Germany have been fascinated by the concept of the *Hörspiel* and have tried to modify or to expand it. Composers certainly saw the similarities between musical and dramatic composition for radio in the early fifties (and some even earlier) so that the concept of audio collages not unlike the experiments with *musique concrète* in France was developed and the results were to be heard in Germany over thirty years ago. It seemed, I suspect, even to the seriously culture-seeking audiences of German radio, to be a specialised and experimental, rather than an archetypal form.

But in the mid-sixties came a movement among young producers and writers throughout the Federal Republic which advocated the establishment of the *Neue Hörspiel* or New Hearplay, which orchestrated speech, music and noise, giving an equal status within the aesthetics of the audio art form to each. It was an exciting and passionate advocacy of pure radio, owing as much to a genuine belief in the nature of the aural experience as to that uneasy reaction to the mid-life crisis which affected all radio organisations at about that time. In the *Neue Hörspiel*, radio writers became in a sense composers, and composers of music certainly became radio writers. The script ceased to be the blueprint for a radio play and those programmes which it was possible to present in script form at all were scripted *after* the production rather than before.

In Britain, it so happened that the revolution in radio programme making came under the Features rather than the Drama department, with the result that much of the innovative use of sound which new technology was making possible in the fifties and sixties took place in programmes other than plays. (What a *feature* actually is has never been satisfactorily defined and would take longer than I have in this short preface to discuss; suffice it that over the years monologues, poems, montages, anthologies, documentaries, compilations and – yes – dramatic narratives have all been presented in feature guise.) Radio Drama itself remained predominantly influenced by the theatrical tradition out of which many members of the BBC's Drama Department had emerged.

The crisis which radio faced then in an acute form was one both of identity and of survival – so perhaps the analogy of the individual's mid-life crisis is an apt one. Faced with the rival attractions of television, the cinema (still, in the fifties, with more than a decade of popularity and commercial success to come) and a proliferation of

living art forms and leisure pursuits, where did radio stand? Was it
a true art form? A mere carrier for the creations of other media?
At worst, perhaps simply a technological stage in the development
of broadcasting – doomed to disappear like the silent movies from
the cinema screen?

Many questioned radio's sometimes hesitant arguments for its own
right to continue to exist; and they weren't only those with vested
interests in other forms.

John Mortimer, having made his début as a dramatist in radio with
The Dock Brief wrote subsequently in the preface to the published
text: 'I do not think that radio drama has achieved any particular
status as an art, nor do I think it will survive, as a dramatic medium,
against the competition of television, except for the performance of
long and rarely done costume dramas of operatic dimensions where
words are all important.' He was writing in 1958 and many people
even in the BBC would have agreed with him. Three years later, as a
young man joining the Drama Department, I was myself very
uncertain whether there was a valid stepping stone, let alone a
career, in this theatre of the mind's eye.

We were, as it turned out, both wrong. While it is true that radio
drama in many parts of the world has declined steadily in both
quality and quantity during the past twenty-five years, in both
Britain and Germany at least it has remained a ubiquitous and
potent ingredient in the broadcasting schedules. However, despite a
certain area of overlap in such universally popular narrative forms as
the thriller (which some would classify separately as 'entertainment'
rather than true 'drama'), it is striking that the moving forces behind
the two most active producers of radio drama in the world have been
divergent ones.

This apparent difference between the writers and producers of the
two nationalities was aired at the last meeting of the European
Broadcasting Union's Drama Experts in Geneva three years ago. As
the assembled delegates – who included many observers from
outside Europe in addition to EBU members – listened to the
demonstrations and descriptions of what each had found their most
satisfying material in recent years, it did indeed seem as if they were
being lured in different directions by rival sirens: Theixepeia, on the
one hand, urging the enchantment of the word in the form of a
traditional narrative; Molpe, perhaps, seductively offering the rival
attraction of song in the form of the *Neue Hörspiel* and its derivatives.
Knowing the argument of old, many delegates thought it both
predictable and insoluble.

Yet as one of the protagonists in the debate, I believe my expert
colleagues to have been mistaken. Although Klaus Schöning – who
spoke for the *Neue Hörspiel* – and I took different approaches to the
subject of radio drama, the distinction between the New and, as it
were, the Old Hearplay is more apparent than real. The fact is that
the *pièce radiophonique*, the emotionally involving creative work

designed for the medium of radio, takes very many forms, and each can influence and enhance the others. There need be no clash between those who see a direct link between the radio experience and the ancient arts of storytelling and spoken verse, and those who believe with Walter Pater, the Victorian essayist and critic, that 'All art constantly aspires towards the condition of music'.

In the heart of a successful radio monologue, or dialogue play, or composite of more abstract sounds, lies the same direct appeal at once to the emotions and to the intellect which is both involving, and intimate, in a way that other media find hard to match. One form of radio may tell us more in concrete detail about people and events; another may inspire deeper and more universal emotions. But these are not separate activities; indeed, they can even be different facets of the same jewel, cut by the same craftsman. Similar arguments occur in the world of painting, between the devotees of traditional and modern art: a late work of Turner or Picasso, if compared with an early work of each master, might tempt one to believe that painting had undergone a one-way revolution; yet there are masterpieces in both periods, and there are outstanding disciples of both. Neither style invalidates the other but rather complements it, testifying to the complexity of human perception and experience.

For contemporary radio writers and producers, there exist two further complications. The first derives from the almost overwhelming availability of information about the state of the world in this age of sophisticated communications technology, which both tempts and bedevils those who have immediate social and political concerns. If radio is to be as vital a medium for the future as undoubtedly it has been for the past sixty years and more, then it must demonstrate its real involvement with the issues which currently confront us. Speaking at the annual meeting of the Radio Academy in 1986, Gillian Reynolds, radio critic of the *Daily Telegraph*, declared that she had learnt more in depth about the situation in Northern Ireland from radio drama than from the news. That's as it should be. News must be confined to reporting the facts, and presenting informed opinion about them. By its nature, it must be concise. Drama, on the other hand, can afford to be more leisurely and to concern itself with the intricacies and contradictions of human nature which alone can hint at an explanation of what are often seemingly illogical events. In many respects our society has become both cynical and impatient – often calling for instant analysis and instant action, yet doubting the validity of either. One solution, often practised, to this dilemma is to move swiftly on to another subject as if to linger were to betray a naïve faith in the efficacy of genuine and serious consideration. Plays have the reverse effect; that is to say that they positively demand pause and reflection, even when their concerns are immediate.

The second complication for the radio playwright lies in the nature of the audience. It has often been pointed out that a radio play is actually only heard by one individual listener, who completes the experience in his or her own imagination. The days of communal listening are very largely over. Yet that individual listener is multiplied several hundred thousand times for each broadcast, with the real possibility that no two responses to the play will be the same. Since the responses are dictated by a great variety of factors – of age and experience, environment, education and mood to name just a few – it follows that writers and producers cannot hope to give equal satisfaction to all, whatever style of programme they decide upon. But in the course of a year, they must be aware that there exists a great variety of tastes.

What a daunting complexity, then, is the contemporary *Hörspiel* – the hearing 'game' which in this country last year achieved an aggregate box-office figure (by adding all the individual audience figures throughout the year) in excess of a staggering 500,000,000 people. Imagination and involvement, poetry, grandeur and gritty realism all had a place in it. So did gentle storytelling in which the message was delivered sometimes subtly by the least perceptible route, sometimes boldly by the front door. At times we laughed or cried or were held in suspense; at others we were mystified or even bored. All the plays broadcast were not of equal quality; yet none was produced that did not have enthusiasm behind it which had brought it to that point; so each played a part in the whole.

The plays in this volume are not – and could not have been – representative of all. As it happens, they are all narrative in form. Whole categories are missing which were widely represented during 1986. Some are missing which were not represented at all. Among those, I must confess, was anything remotely resembling a *Neue Hörspiel*. And that's a pity. But it makes one more target for writers and producers in 1987. For the Old Hearplay is quite capable of playing host to the New, and finding in its content and techniques ways of enriching the experience of the listener (and perhaps causing problems to the publisher of this volume) in years to come.

Richard Imison
(February 1987)

DREAMS, SECRETS, BEAUTIFUL LIES

by Robert Ferguson

To Nina Elisabeth Normann

Robert Ferguson grew up near Blackpool in Lancashire and left school in 1968. He worked until 1976 and then began studying at UCL for a degree in Scandinavian Studies, specialising in Norwegian. In 1983 he went to Norway on a scholarship from the Norwegian government and now lives there. His biography of Knut Hamsun was published earlier this year. In 1984 he won the Giles Cooper Award for his play *Transfigured Night*.

Dreams, Secrets, Beautiful Lies was first broadcast on BBC Radio 3 on 2 April 1986. The cast was as follows:

PAMELA	Diana Quick
EDWARD	Charles Kay
EMILY	Emma Glasner
SHOPKEEPER	Ellen McIntosh
GRAVEDIGGER	Alan Thompson

Director: Richard Imison
Running time, as broadcast: 73 minutes, 21 seconds

1

PAMELA *is on the phone,* EMILY *is upstairs.*

PAMELA. I can't, what would I say, what excuse could I give? . . . No
I can't say that. Anyway it's too late, I've already said I'll go . . .
Look, I feel guilty enough as it is. God how I hate this creeping
about and telling lies . . . Oh come on how could I have, how
could I have? – 'No I'm sorry I'm not in a position to consider
moving to a new house in the country because as a matter of fact
I'm leaving you next Monday, perhaps I should've mentioned it
before' . . . Yes I'm all right, it's just that I wish there was another
way. Why does it all have to be such a mess? . . . Listen, um,
maybe we should put it off for a couple of weeks. Just postpone it
for a couple of weeks . . . Oh don't take it like that for God's sake
. . . Of course I do, of course I love you. I was only wondering if it
might not be a better idea to postpone it. Just until this is over. I
mean I had no idea he was going to come up with all this . . . No,
nothing, you know what he's like, he keeps everything secret.
He doesn't even know he's doing it, he's always been like that.
It doesn't even occur to him that other people might have plans . . .
Mm, mm . . . I know, I know . . . I know but it's just that
everything seems to be happening at once at the moment . . . No
it isn't that, he hasn't a clue, I'm certain of it. But I sometimes
wonder if Emily . . . well it's the way she looks at me sometimes.
I catch her staring at me in such a queer way sometimes . . . I know,
I know, you're right, I know it's just paranoia. Listen, I told you
didn't I, that Edward thinks she's psychic? (*She laughs rather
hysterically.*) You know what? You know what I wish? I wish you'd
come round here right now and make love to me. Right here on
the rug here. I feel I just want to . . . This is killing me, you know.
It's killing me. Sometimes when I'm at work, or when I'm having
breakfast, or on the tube, it doesn't matter where it is, sometimes

I feel I just want to stop whatever it is I'm doing and stand up and open my mouth and . . .

EMILY (*upstairs, calling*). Mum. Mum.

PAMELA (*turning to call back*). Emily? Is that you?

EMILY. I can't find my *Pears Cyclopaedia.*

PAMELA. Have you looked in your room?

EMILY. Yes of course I've looked in my room.

PAMELA. I'll be up in a minute love, I'm just on the phone. (*Into the phone.*) Listen, I'll have to go now. You are going to the party tonight aren't you? We can talk about it then. I think maybe we should postpone it. Just for a couple of weeks. Until this is over. Bye.

She hangs up.

EMILY. Who was that?

PAMELA. I didn't hear you come in Emily. You gave me such a fright.

EMILY. I came in the back. Who were you speaking to?

PAMELA. You mind your own business who I was speaking to. Where've you looked for this encyclopaedia?

EMILY. Everywhere.

PAMELA (*runs up the stairs*). I'll bet. (*Into* EMILY's *room.*) Right: where've you looked?

EMILY. I just told you – everywhere.

PAMELA (*beginning to look*). Honestly, look at the state of this room. It's a wonder you can even find your bed in it.

EMILY. I've already looked in the cupboard.

PAMELA. Well we'll just look again shall we?

EMILY. Where are we going tomorrow? Edward won't tell me. He says it's a secret.

PAMELA. I thought you liked secrets.

EMILY. I do, sometimes. But where are we going?

PAMELA. We're going to drive out to the country and look at a house.

EMILY. For us?

PAMELA. Yes.

EMILY. Might we be moving?

PAMELA. What's this?

EMILY. That's not it. Why might we be moving?

PAMELA. Edward wants to move. He says he doesn't want to live in London anymore. He wants to go and live in the country with all the sheep and the insects. (*She finds a book.*) Is this it?

EMILY. Oh yeah. I never saw it.

PAMELA. You mean you never looked.

EMILY. Yes I did. I just didn't look there.

PAMELA. Look harder.

EMILY. I did look harder. Maybe it wasn't there before.

PAMELA. Emily.

EMILY. Who were you talking to?

PAMELA. Emily were you listening to my private telephone conversation?

EMILY. No.

PAMELA. Because it's very rude, that is – listening when other people are having a private conversation. It's what they call eavesdropping.

EMILY. I wasn't listening. I can't help hearing if you're on the phone. Was it Michael?

PAMELA. No it wasn't Michael. It was a colleague of mine from work. They're having a jumble sale and he wanted to know if there was anything we could give him.

EMILY. Oh. (*Pause.*) Will you be late at this party tonight?

PAMELA. Not too late. Carol's babysitting and she's got to be back home by twelve o'clock.

EMILY. Oh no, not Carol.

PAMELA. Don't say that, Carol's very nice.

EMILY. Yeah, she's very nice, she's just stupid, that's all.

PAMELA. No she isn't. I think Carol's a very intelligent girl. Why do you say she's stupid?

EMILY. Because she is. She says the Shroud of Turin is just some monk's rotten old T-shirt.

PAMELA. Who's been talking to you about the Shroud of Turin?

EMILY. Edward. He showed me a picture of it.

PAMELA. Yes, I thought it might've been him.

EMILY. It's Jesus' face after he was crucified. You can see it.

PAMELA. Yes, I know what the Shroud of Turin is. (*Pause.*) Why don't you ask Carol when she comes if she'll help you tidy up your room?

EMILY. I don't want it tidied up. I like it like this. (*Pause.*) What jumble did you tell this man he could have for his jumble sale?

PAMELA. Oh I haven't thought. A few old clothes. (*Going downstairs.*) The table in the garden maybe. The old washing machine. I haven't thought.

EMILY. Don't give the old washing machine away.

PAMELA (*downstairs*). Why not, lovey?

EMILY. Because I don't want you to.

PAMELA. But it doesn't work anymore.

EMILY. I know. But I like it.

PAMELA. But if it doesn't work, love. What's the use of keeping it if it doesn't work?

EMILY. I *like* it for not working. That's *why* I like it. You're not to give it away. It's not fair.

PAMELA. Emily don't shout at me, I'm only downstairs, I'm not out in the street.

EMILY (*shouting*). I'm not shouting at you.

PAMELA. Emily!

EMILY. Go away. Leave me alone. (*She slams the door of her room.*)

2

Driving through the countryside the following day. EDWARD *driving.* PAMELA *beside him.* EMILY *in the back.*

PAMELA. What's the name of the place again? There's ten places here all with identical names. Clunton, Clunbury, Clun, Clungunford, Clingunford, Clongonford, Clangunford, Clunk.

EDWARD. Clungunford. I've marked it with a traditional 'X'. We want the Ludlow road.

PAMELA. In that case we should've taken a left at the last crossing.

EDWARD. I'll take the next left when we come to it.

PAMELA. There isn't one.

EDWARD. There's bound to be. Emily, what should you do if your ear goes bald?

EMILY. If your ear goes *bald*? How can your *ear* go bald?

PAMELA. Edward, I am looking at the map and there is no left turn. You'll have to take the B.4367 at Aston and turn left there.

EMILY. How can a person's ear go bald?

EDWARD. What about that turn there?

PAMELA. That's a private road.

EMILY. Are we lost?

PAMELA. } Yes.
EDWARD. } Not really.

EMILY. In my book of map and compass it tells you how you can point your watch at the sun and tell which way is north from the hour hand.

EDWARD. Come on then, which way is north?

EMILY. You can't do it with this, this is a digital watch.

EDWARD. Ask it then. Ask it which way is north. I thought they could speak, those digital watches.

EMILY. Ha ha.

EDWARD. Imagine that. She gets a wristwatch free with a five-litre tin of engine oil. What progress we've made since the days of football cards and plastic submarines.

PAMELA. Yeah the good old days, head lice and rickets and powdered egg, no milk in your tea and the books printed on toilet paper.

EMILY. The Indian where we got this said he had one just the same and it went for three months.

EDWARD. Yes, wasn't that wonderful? (*Pause.*) You see those hills over there on the right, those are the Stretton Hills. And there's the legendary Wenlock Edge there. I was talking to a chap at the party last night who believes there's gold in Wenlock Edge. He was talking about buying it and digging it all up. Emily, you can see two counties from here at exactly the same time. Worcestershire and Shropshire. (*Pause.*) Emily?

EMILY. What?

EDWARD. I've just told you a very interesting fact.

EMILY. Yes I know. Listen to this: (*Reading:*) 'Eleven Days – Give Us Back Our Eleven Days: When England adopted the Gregorian Calendar by Chesterfield's Act of 1751 in place of the Julian Calendar, eleven days were dropped, so that Wednesday, 2 September 1752 was followed by Thursday, 14 September.' Well, how could they *do* that? Listen: (*Reads on:*) 'This has given rise to a double computation as, Lady Day, 25 March/Old Lady Day, 6 April; Midsummer Day, 24 June/Old Midsummer Day, 6 July; Christmas Day, 25 December/Old Christmas Day, 6 January.' Well, how can they *do* that?

EDWARD. What's this in aid of?

EMILY. It's my homework. I'm supposed to be doing this thing about calendars. This girl Sunita's doing about Indian calendars and I'm doing about English ones. It's for tomorrow. How can they do that?

EDWARD. It means that the days between the 2nd and the 14th were dropped from the calendar. Wednesday was still followed by Thursday, but the numbered days in between were dropped.

EMILY. But suppose it was today. You know, 10 September, only in 1752. Well how could it be?

EDWARD. These days never actually existed, Emily. It's not as if they passed, and then the government came along afterwards and took them away again – they never existed at all. They just never came. There *was* no today. There *was* no 10 September.

EMILY. There must've been. Otherwise how can anything be real? Suppose when we look at the house and we decide to buy it and then afterwards when we go back it just isn't *there* anymore. Well how could you prove *anything* that happened today?

EDWARD. A calendar isn't such a very important thing, you know. All it is really is a piece of paper with numbers on. It's a tool for measuring time with, that's all. It isn't time itself.

EMILY. Could they do it again?

EDWARD. Yes they could, unfortunately.

EMILY. But what about Christmas Day? How could they move Christmas Day?

EDWARD. By pretending it's just an ordinary day, just another number on the calendar. Not Christmas Day, just 25 December.

EMILY. But it's Jesus' birthday. That's *why* it's Christmas Day.

EDWARD. Yes but, you know, he wasn't actually born on Christmas Day.

EMILY. Yes he was.

PAMELA. No he wasn't born on Christmas Day, love, that's just a tradition. (*To* EDWARD.) You want a left here.

The car slows.

EMILY. He *was* born on Christmas Day.

EDWARD. I know it seems confusing, Emily. Try to understand that there's no such thing as reality. It's just a word. People have to speak, and they need something to say, so they make up words.

PAMELA. Edward for God's sake! I don't think you're explaining this very well.

EDWARD. Well I should hope not. What usually happens, Emily, is that people agree to things happening without actually understanding why they happen. We accept things. It makes life easier.

EMILY. But it says here there were riots, and the people wanted the eleven days back because they thought the government had stolen them.

PAMELA. It's because they weren't very bright, love. They didn't try to work it out. You have to work things out. You have to get out your pencil and paper and work things out. You can't expect to understand things if you can't be bothered to work them out.

EDWARD. Look over there. That must be the steeple at Hughley. The legendary steeple at Hughley.

EMILY. Edward look out!

He brakes sharply and the car halts.

EDWARD. I didn't hit him did I?

EMILY. He ran into the trees there! I saw him! It was a fox!

PAMELA. I thought it was a dog.

EMILY. It was a fox! Wasn't it, Edward!

EDWARD. I don't know, I didn't really see it, I just saw a sort of streak.

PAMELA. It was a dog. A brown dog. A labrador or something.

EMILY. It was a fox!

EDWARD. Emily, don't shout like that. It goes right through my head.

EMILY (*subsiding*). It was a fox. It was.

The car starts moving again.

EDWARD (*as they drive on*). Well whatever it was we didn't hit him.

EMILY. Anyway we *did* see a fox last week. Lydia and me.

PAMELA. In London?

EMILY. Of course it was in London, where else did you think it would be, by the seaside? (*Pause.*) It was in a bin along Half Moon Lane. We saw it when we were coming back from school.

EDWARD. What was it doing in the bin?

EMILY. It was dead, stupid.

PAMELA. Don't talk to Edward like that please, Emily.

EMILY. Sorry. (*Pause.*) But I *said*. I *said* it was in a bin. Why else would it be in a bin?

EDWARD. Emily . . .

EMILY. Sorry.

3

Later. The car draws up in the village and EDWARD *turns off the engine.*

EDWARD. That looks like it there – antiques shop facing the cricket pavilion with a blue sunblind.

PAMELA. It's more like what I'd call a junk shop – look at the state of that wardrobe there.

EMILY. Can we come in with you?

EDWARD. It's not worth it. I'm only picking up the key. The house isn't here, it's in the next village.

PAMELA. How far away is that?

EDWARD. Eight or nine miles by road.

EMILY. Why does the owner live so far away from his shop?

EDWARD. She doesn't live there. The house belonged to her mother. I think she's put her in a home. (*He opens the car door.*) Or perhaps she died. (*He gets out.*) Shan't be long. (*He shuts the door and walks to the shop.*)

PAMELA. I hope he isn't long. What's the time?

EMILY. It's exactly (*Pause.*) ten to three. (*Pause.*) What are those men doing with that roller?

PAMELA. They're rolling the cricket pitch. It's for cricket. Wind your window up, there's a love.

EMILY. Why? It's hot.

PAMELA. Because I don't like the smell, that's why.

EMILY (*winding it up*). OK. (*Pause.*) I hope we get this house you know.

PAMELA. You haven't even seen it yet. Suppose you don't like it?

EMILY. I will like it. Edward described it to me.

PAMELA. He hasn't seen it yet either.

EMILY. Yes but he's seen a brochure from the estate agents. (*Pause.*) Mum . . .

PAMELA. Mm?

EMILY. Do you think it's wrong to pray for things you want just for yourself?

PAMELA. No, I don't think it's wrong, I just don't think it does any good. Why?

EMILY. Because according to the brochure there's a field at the back of the house where you can keep a horse, and I was wondering if it would be all right to pray to get a horse?

PAMELA. Well you can try, but I don't think it'll do you much good. It costs money to keep a horse you know, and God doesn't know anything about money. (*Pause.*) Don't you like living in London, Em? I thought you liked it there.

EMILY. Well I do, but I'd rather live in the country.

PAMELA. I think the country's a bit boring. It's just hay and animals, and old men with red faces and dirty little hats on. Don't you think you might get fed up with it?

EMILY. I dunno. Maybe. But in the country people don't shout all the time, do they?

PAMELA. How d'you mean?

EMILY. You know. Shout.

PAMELA. Who shouts? Who d'you mean?

EMILY. People. You know, people. They shout at night.

PAMELA. Well I've never heard anything. (*Pause.*) You won't be too disappointed if for some reason or other we can't have this house, will you?

EMILY. Will you be?

PAMELA. It might make life very difficult for me. I mean, for me to get to London in time for work at nine I'll have to get up about six o'clock every morning. And I wouldn't get back until about seven or eight o'clock in the evening. I might even have to stay overnight sometimes. Who'll look after you? Who'll get your meals for you?

EMILY. Edward. He does anyway.

PAMELA. Sometimes. (*Pause.*) You'd have to change schools you know. Wouldn't you miss your friends? Lydia, and Susan Reynolds, and Chaka, and Ben Jamal?

EMILY. They could come out and visit at weekends.

PAMELA. They might do, love, but I wouldn't bet on it. People say they're going to keep up with you but they never do. Half the time they don't even notice you've gone away until you come back again. (*Pause.*) What's he doing in there? Can you see him. He's only supposed to be picking up a key.

EMILY. He's talking to the woman. Maybe he knows her from when he used to live round here.

PAMELA. Edward never used to live round here. When did he used to live round here?

EMILY. I don't know, probably when he was younger.

PAMELA. No he didn't. What makes you think that?

EMILY. Well the way he knows all these hills and that. I thought he might have lived here before he met us, when he had his other wife.

PAMELA. No love, I think you've got hold of the wrong end of the stick. I expect he just knows it from the map. (*Pause.*) Jesus, we're never going to get there.

EMILY. We've got plenty of time, it's only (*Pause.*) one minute past three.

PAMELA. I know. But I've got a lot of packing to do this evening.

EMILY. What time is your plane tomorrow?

PAMELA. You what, love?

EMILY. What time is your plane?

PAMELA. Four o'clock.

EMILY. Mum, when you go, can I come and see you off?

PAMELA. No you can't. It would be nice darling, but you won't be back in time from school.

EMILY. But I want to see you off.

PAMELA. It's out of the question, Emily.

EMILY. But I want to see you when you get on the plane. I want to make sure you get on it.

PAMELA. I'll be all right. Now just be quiet please.

EMILY. But I want to see you get on it.

PAMELA. Emily, don't shout. You're always shouting. (*Pause.*) Anyway I might not go. I'm not sure yet.

EMILY. I hope you don't. It's such a long way. I know it's stupid but, sometimes if I can't get to sleep at night, or I get woken up suddenly, when I look in my head I always see an aeroplane flying along. Even when I don't want to, you know, I can still see it. Even when I keep my eyes open. And then after about five seconds it always starts falling down and down towards the sea, and it doesn't matter how hard I try, I can never make it keep flying.

PAMELA (*hugs her*). Emily, come here. Emily sweet. My sweet, sweet Emily. You mustn't have dreams like that. Promise me you won't. Ever again. Listen: I want to buy you something very special. Next weekend we'll go out shopping together, just you and me. We'll go to the big toyshop down Regent's Street, and we'll get you something really special. But you must promise me first not to think about this plane again. OK?

EMILY. OK.

PAMELA. That's a promise. I promise you.

EMILY. Thanks. (*Fading.*) Those little children are trying to tie a white sun-hat on their poodle, but it doesn't want them to . . .

4

Joining Edward in the shop.

EDWARD. So we go through the churchyard, and it's a house on the far side, overlooking the green, with a white picket fence.

SHOPKEEPER. There's two apple trees in the front garden. You'll see that some of the stones on the front of the house have been picked out in yellow and blue paint.

EDWARD. It sounds utterly charming. Was she an artist, your mother?

SHOPKEEPER. No, she just liked to brighten things up a bit with her paintbrush.

EDWARD. Yes indeed, you must miss her very much. Now, you did give me the key, didn't you? Yes, that's right, here it is, in my pocket. I'll drop it by later on today.

SHOPKEEPER. If I'm not in, you can just pop it through the letter-box.

EDWARD (*winding up a musical box and setting it playing*). I say, this is rather nice.

SHOPKEEPER. It's a snuff box. Eighteenth century. Made by Samuel Pemberton of Birmingham. It has a Swiss, radial-type movement.

EDWARD. Well I'm damned. What a lot you know about these things. It's a wonderful sound, isn't it? So frail and ethereal and remote. (*Pause. He wanders further.*) What wonderful things you have here! Look at this magnificent sword!

SHOPKEEPER. That sword was carried at the Battle of Inkerman, in the Crimean War. It's about 130 years old.

EDWARD. Was it really? And it's still sharp. (*Wandering further.*) Oh you must love it here, surrounded by all these lovely, dusty, smelly old things. Look at this splendid old rocking-horse. Just the thing for a breezy gallop when trade's a bit slack.

SHOPKEEPER. It's not in working order. One of the rockers is broken. Here.

EDWARD. So it is. What a pity. (*The music stops.*) Where did you get this?

SHOPKEEPER. What?

EDWARD. This picture. This photograph of a girl in a white dress.

SHOPKEEPER. I don't know. My husband was over at Clun the other day clearing a house and he brought back three tea chests full of books and diaries and old photographs. I think that was probably one of them.

EDWARD. How much do you want for it?

SHOPKEEPER. Oh I don't know, give me 50p.

EDWARD. 50p? I should think the frame alone is worth £5. What are you running, Mrs Finzi – a business or a charity shop?

SHOPKEEPER. Well give me what you like for it.

EDWARD. My dear Mrs Finzi I despair of you. It'll have to be £5 anyway, I haven't got anything smaller.

SHOPKEEPER. I can change it, if you like.

EDWARD. Nonononononononono.

SHOPKEEPER. Well if you're sure.

EDWARD (*moving off*). Quite sure. Cheerio.

SHOPKEEPER. Cheerio.

Cut to exterior. EDWARD *closes the shop door and walks to the car.*

PAMELA. What kept you? You were only supposed to be picking up the key.

EDWARD (*approaching*). Sorry. (*He opens the car door.*) Fascinating woman. Do you know what she does when she gets bored? (*He gets in and shuts the door.*) She shuts up the shop, sets all the musical boxes playing and then she climbs up onto that rocking horse with an old sword tied round her waist, and makes believe that she is a woman general riding into battle against the forces of darkness. And of course, she insisted on demonstrating all this nonsense for me. (*Giving* EMILY *the picture.*) Look after this for me Emily.

EMILY. Who is it?

EDWARD. It's a woman in a white dress.

EMILY. I can see that. Is she famous?

EDWARD. What does that matter? She's just a very beautiful woman.

PAMELA. Let's have a look. Pass it over, Emily.

EMILY. Here. (*Passing it.*) Her face is ever so pale.

PAMELA (*Pause*). I don't like her face. She looks secretive. Her face is like a mask. There's no expression on it.

EDWARD. Who asked for your opinion?

PAMELA. Let's just get going shall we?

EDWARD *turns the engine over, but there is only a 'clunk'.*

EDWARD. I think the starter motor's gone.

PAMELA. Oh Jesus.

EDWARD. Just be patient.

Another and another clunk.

PAMELA. Keep trying. Try harder.

EDWARD. Pamela, for God's sake I'm turning the key, how can I try harder to turn a key? (*Another clunk.*) No.

PAMELA (*fading*). Jesus wept . . .

5

Later. At the bed and breakfast farmhouse in Clungunford. EMILY *has her own room across a corridor, and* PAMELA *and* EDWARD *have a sitting-room with a bedroom off. We're in the sitting-room. The window is open.*

PAMELA. Jesus, what a place. Did you see the size of that commode in Emily's room? She should have a lifebelt on the wall in case someone falls down it. Are you sure there were no rooms at the hotel?

EDWARD. Yes. There's a cricket team on tour – all the rooms are taken. This is fine, I like this. (*He laughs.*) She asked me who was having the double room. She must've thought you and Emily were my daughters.

PAMELA. She wants her eyes testing if she does, you don't look that old. (*She sighs.*) Oh what a drag. Are you sure there's no garages open?

EDWARD. Pam, he opens at eight tomorrow, we'll be on the road again by nine. It's only a starter motor, it won't take him long. We can drive back via Clun and take a look at the house on the way. We should be back in London mid-morning. What time is your flight?

PAMELA. Four.

EDWARD. You'll have plenty of time.

PAMELA. Will you be going on into work?

EDWARD. Have to. I can drop Emily off at school on the way. Unless you want me to take you to the airport?

PAMELA. No, no, that's all right. (PAMELA *throws herself down on the bed.*) God this bed's hard. (*Sniffs.*) It's got a very funny smell.

I think it's damp. Maybe I should take out a little mirror and hold it just above the sheets.

EDWARD (*tutting at the window*). Chap here's just gone in to bat wearing a pair of ordinary brown walking-shoes. I don't know, what's happening to this country, Pamela? Come over here a moment, I want to show you something.

PAMELA. Edward, I'm just having a lie-down.

EDWARD. Come and look.

PAMELA (*coming*). It's not this man's shoes, is it?

EDWARD. No not that. You see those hills over there?

PAMELA. What hills?

EDWARD. There. Where my finger's pointing. Above the tree and to the left of the church tower. Just in line with the clock.

PAMELA (*pause*). Those are just clouds.

EDWARD. No they're not. That's the Clent and Lickey Hills. And over there in the west look – come round this side of me – those are the Shropshire Hills.

PAMELA (*yawns*). Oh yeah. It looks like the design you did for BMP. (*She returns to the bed.*) Oh God, I'm so tired.

EDWARD. I don't think it looks like my design.

PAMELA. Yes it does, it looks exactly like it. You want to get onto them about those, you know. It's time you heard something. Get onto them, tell them you want a decision.

EDWARD. They gave me a decision.

The dull thud of a ball on a pad. Appeals for lbw.

PAMELA. What did they say?

EDWARD. They're not using them.

PAMELA. Oh Edward. When did you hear?

EDWARD. Oh I forget. About ten days ago.

PAMELA. Oh Edward.

EDWARD. What do you mean, 'Oh Edward'? Stop saying 'Oh Edward' like that. You sound like the bloody Queen.

PAMELA. But you worked hard on them.

EDWARD. No I did not. I did not work hard on them. I don't know the meaning of the word work. (*Pause.*) Anyway, I knew quite well when I did them that they wouldn't use them.

PAMELA. Well then excuse me for asking but why did you bother doing them in the first place?

EDWARD. I don't know, for fun. Why does anybody do anything?

PAMELA. Well it's not usually for fun I can tell you that. Why didn't you tell me?

EDWARD. It's not very interesting.

PAMELA. But they meant a lot to you. You said yourself they were the best things you've ever done.

EDWARD. I always say that. It doesn't mean anything.

PAMELA. Did they give you a reason?

EDWARD. They said they were old-fashioned, if you call that a reason. Fashion. What the hell has fashion got to do with it? It's just a word, it doesn't mean anything.

PAMELA. Fashion is a fact of life.

EDWARD. So am I a fact of life, I don't necessarily mean anything.

PAMELA. Well anyway, I hope you're not too upset.

EDWARD. Of course I'm not upset. Don't be ridiculous. As a matter of fact I'm glad. It'll give me more time for my tattooing.

PAMELA. Your tattooing?

EDWARD. Didn't I tell you? I'm going into partnership with Vic, the security guard at Polletts. We're going to run a mobile service tattooing boiled eggs for the idle rich. Vic's doing the boiling, and I'll be handling the creative side of things.

PAMELA. Well since you're in such a practical frame of mind perhaps you'd tell me where you intend getting the money to buy a place round here. Anything round here is going to cost a fortune. I wish you'd never thought of it.

EDWARD. Don't worry. Everything'll be all right.

PAMELA (*snorts*). Have you got a cigarette?

EDWARD. In my jacket pocket. On the back of the chair. (*Pause.*) It's a lovely name, Clungunford. It's like lying in a field on a Sunday morning, and hearing a bell ringing in the distance. Housman used it in 'A Shropshire Lad'.

PAMELA. What's 'A Shropshire Lad'?

EDWARD. You work for the largest publishing company in Great Britain and you've never heard of 'A Shropshire Lad'?

PAMELA. Apparently not. What is it?

EDWARD. It's a poem.

PAMELA. Sounds like the name of a pub. (*Resuming the bed with her cigarette.*) God, this bed is just unsleepable-on. (*Pause.*) What time did you leave the party last night? Michael said you went early. Weren't you enjoying yourself?

EDWARD. No. The hostess refused to let me play my Shirley Bassey record.

PAMELA. Why didn't you tell me you were going? You're so bloody secretive.

EDWARD. I couldn't find you.

PAMELA. I was probably in the kitchen. I got waylaid by some bloke who was telling me about sexual perversions among the ancient Greeks. Apparently they used to screw statues, the dirty sods. Agalosomething. Agalopholia or something.

EDWARD. Was he trying to pick you up?

PAMELA. Was who trying to pick me up?

EDWARD. This bloke. This bloke at the party. Was he trying to pick you up?

PAMELA. No, he was a psychologist. It's not as common as it used to be apparently. Your modern man's more into plastic dolls.

EDWARD. The effects of plastic on our civilisation have been incalculable. (*The church clock is heard ringing.*) It's four o'clock. How about a walk? Why don't we walk over and take a look at the house this afternoon? We could ask the landlady if she'll do us a late supper.

PAMELA. I thought you said it was about eight miles.

EDWARD. That's by road. (*Pause.*) There are footpaths through the fields. I saw them on the map. I should think they cut it down to about half the distance.

PAMELA. We still haven't got time.

EDWARD. Come on, it's a lovely afternoon. It wouldn't really matter if we got there or not.

PAMELA. Of course it would matter. What's the point of going somewhere if you don't get there?

EDWARD. Don't shout. There's no need to shout.

PAMELA. I'm not shouting. (*Pause.*) I'm sorry. I'm tired and I'm pissed off. You go. Take Emily with you and you can tell me what it's like when you get back. I've got work to do.

EDWARD. Where is Emily?

PAMELA. She's downstairs talking to Mrs Whatsername.

EDWARD. Are you sure you won't come?

PAMELA. Quite sure. Pass me that manuscript will you? The pink folder on the dresser.

EDWARD. She's a very sensible woman, our landlady. She's never been to Shrewsbury in her life. This one?

PAMELA. Yes. Pass it over.

EMILY (*reads*). 'Abdul slipped the wriggling little fish in between the slippery lips of her vagina and sat back, observing the girl with a smile. "Does it feel good?" he whispered, as he watched the little yellow tail delicately twitching back and forth between her pale thighs. The girl sighed and nodded, unable to speak. Her whole body, glistening with sweat, was moving convulsively, undulating and twisting on the cool silken sheets. Her lips twitched and stretched as the little tail flickered and flexed inside her, sending icy sparks of electricity flashing through her body. Suddenly Abdul stood up and put on his jacket.

"Where are you going?" she moaned. "Oh God don't go, don't go now."

"I'll be back in a minute," said Abdul, "I'm just going out for some chips".'

PAMELA. Give it here please.

EDWARD. Are you going to publish this?

PAMELA. I don't know yet.

EDWARD. What's it supposed to be about?

PAMELA. Sex. I wouldn't expect you to like it. Give it to me please.

EDWARD. Here. Your author knows as much about sex as a pig does about oranges.

PAMELA. Oh yeah? And what the hell do you know about sex?

EDWARD. We'll see you later. We shouldn't be too late.

6

Later. PAMELA *talking on the telephone.*

PAMELA. It's the starter or something. We'll be back mid-morning tomorrow. Emily and Edward have gone to look at the house . . . I said I had work to do, which is the truth, I do. Oh God it's good to talk to you. I feel so damn nervous all the time. I keep thinking I'm going to be sick . . . Here? Two rooms. A sort of sitting-room and a bedroom. Emily's got her own room . . . It's very pretty. Sort of olde worlde. There's a village green with people playing cricket. Mostly stockbrokers I expect. There's even a duck-pond with real ducks on it . . . What? . . . Yeah, I suppose it is, if you're about 89 years old and you like a quiet life . . . No, much better, much better. I feel stronger. I feel kind-of more (*Pause.*) distanced. I feel as though it isn't really me, I'm watching myself. The awful thing is that sometimes I feel proud of myself. Of how well I'm doing it. I mean, I've not had any rehearsals you know.

Oh God I'm so glad you were in. Do you ever worry about going insane? . . . All right then, not insane, but just losing control. Say, you break down and cry and you can't do anything about it. Or you sit down in a chair and then find you can't get up again . . . (*She laughs.*) No, no. That's the weird thing. It's like I said, I almost feel as though I'm an actress, and I'm very sure of the part I'm playing, I've got a great belief in it and I want to play it well, I want to play it to the best of my ability, I want to make it work . . . Mm, mm. But what happens with me . . . Mm, mm. What happens with me is that when I'm alone in a room with a mirror I go and stand in front of it and I force myself to look into my own eyes, I stare and stare at them for minutes on end. It's as if I'm scared to look away. I started doing it just now, after they'd gone out. I went into the bedroom to get my bag and I caught my reflection in the mirror and I sat down and began staring at myself and, after a while, after maybe three minutes, the room behind me and everything in the mirror began to sort-of waver about. Everything turned black. It was like there was a halo of blackness round me. The only thing I could still recognise were my own eyes. I felt as if I was a , I don't know, I was like some kind of animal, like a wolf . . . (*She laughs.*) I know, yeah. And me a bloody vegetarian . . . Guilt, I suppose. Don't worry, I can handle it. But d'you know what? D'you know what I really wish? I really wish he'd be nastier. I wish he'd hit me or something. I think I'd feel better about it. Oh don't listen to me, take no notice of me, I don't know what I'm saying. I don't know, sometimes I wonder if there's something the matter with me. Maybe there's some higher form of maturity I'd discover if I stopped thinking about (*Pause.*) I don't know, God, I think I'd have to stop thinking about 90 per cent of the things I think about if I really wanted to change. I'm stuck with my desires. That's all there is to it – I *am* my desires. Love, I better go now, I've got to get this manuscript finished. Listen: I've decided to tell him . . . That was yesterday, I was a wreck yesterday. I know you're only saying that because you're thinking of me. But I've been thinking about it. It's my life, and I don't want to go sneaking out of my own past like a dog, with notes stuck on the bathroom mirror and all that bollocks. That was how my mother did it, you know. I never felt it was right. I couldn't respect her for it . . . No I've made up my mind, I'm going to tell him tonight.

7

EDWARD *and* EMILY *at the next village.*

EDWARD. Well I don't understand this at all: there's the churchyard, there's the green – where's the house with the painted stones and the apple trees in the front garden?

EMILY. Maybe she meant it's back on the other side of the churchyard.

EDWARD. But we've just come from the other side of the churchyard.

EMILY. Ask that man over there, he might know.

EDWARD. What man?

EMILY. There. In the cemetery. Digging underneath that tree.

EDWARD. Good idea. We'll go and ask him.

They enter the cemetery; the sound of the gate, and gravel path.

Close the gate behind you!

EMILY (*closes the gate*). OK. Wait. Don't go so fast!

EDWARD. You're not afraid are you?

EMILY. No. Of course I'm not afraid.

EDWARD. The dead are nothing to be afraid of – some of the best people in England are dead. See how nicely they keep their little patches of ground. This chap's put a little statue of a pigeon up on top of his stone.

EMILY. It's a dove, isn't it? (*Pause.*) Did you know that Mum's going to give away the old washing machine for a jumble sale? I heard her talking to a man on the phone.

EDWARD. No, I hadn't heard that.

EMILY. You won't let her, will you?

EDWARD. Why not? It doesn't work, it's rusty, it's full of rain.

EMILY. Well if nobody else can use it what's the point of giving it away? Why don't we just keep it?

EDWARD. There's not much point in anybody having it really.

EMILY. I like it. I've always liked it. I liked it when it worked and I like it now and I always will like it. Don't chuck it away, will you?

EDWARD. OK. I'll see if we can get a preservation order slapped on it.

EMILY. Maybe we could take it with us when we move. I could clean it up and have it in my room.

The sound of digging.

EDWARD. If your room's big enough. If we ever reach the house to find out if it's big enough. (*To the* GRAVEDIGGER:) Excuse me, do you know where Byron Cottage is?

GRAVEDIGGER. Byron Cottage? What's the name of the people?

EDWARD. There's no one living there at the moment. I think the owner's name was probably Lambert. An old lady.

GRAVEDIGGER. Lambert? No, I don't think so.

EDWARD. It has a white fence. A white fence. Some of the stones are painted yellow and blue. It faces across the green, towards St Cecilia's.

GRAVEDIGGER. St Cecilia's? You've got the wrong church, my friend – this is St Antony's. You want Clun.

EDWARD. This is Clun.

GRAVEDIGGER. Clunton.

EDWARD. Are you sure?

GRAVEDIGGER. 'Course I'm sure – I was born here.

EMILY. Edward . . .

EDWARD. Emily be quiet. (*To the* GRAVEDIGGER:) I'm afraid I don't understand.

EMILY. Edward . . .

EDWARD. Emily, just go away and play a moment. I'm trying to talk to this gentleman.

EMILY. OK . . .

GRAVEDIGGER. You must've took a wrong turning. Where've you just come from?

EDWARD. We've just walked over from Clungunford. We used the footpaths. I'm certain it said Clun on the signpost.

GRAVEDIGGER. Oh you came that way did you? Yes, I know the sign you mean. It wants replacing. The end bit's fallen off it. It should say Clunton.

EDWARD. Oh I see. Clunton. Clunton. It never occurred to me.

GRAVEDIGGER. Well it wouldn't, would it. You're looking to buy this house are you?

EDWARD. Yes, if we can find it.

GRAVEDIGGER. There's a place for sale here. Old Patrick Hadley's place. There behind the post office over there. Council got him a flat in town near his married daughter. You want to look at that, that's a nice little place.

EDWARD. I'm sure it is. But it has to be Clun.

GRAVEDIGGER. I see. You got family out that way?

EDWARD. No, it isn't that. I used to know the area vaguely. When I was at art school I had a friend who lived there. Her parents had a farm and I stayed there one summer. Long time ago now. You know, I thought I didn't quite recognise the village, but things change so much, people knock old buildings down, put new ones up . . . I thought my memory was playing tricks on me. Do you know Clun at all?

GRAVEDIGGER. Yes, I've got a brother lives over there.

EDWARD. There was a grey house there covered in ivy, overlooking the green. It had an ornamental pond in the garden, and a marble statue of a woman. Is that still there?

GRAVEDIGGER. Mr Sharman's place? Yes, that's still there. Was that the people you knew?

EDWARD. No, I didn't know them. I didn't know the Sharman family. Emily!

EMILY. Coming.

EDWARD. Thank you for your help. Goodbye.

GRAVEDIGGER. Good luck.

EMILY (*rejoining* EDWARD *as he walks on*). Edward, there was a boy there that was run over who was born on exactly the same date as me. The same year and everything. But even though we were born at exactly the same time, I'm older than him. It's queer isn't it?

EDWARD. Yes it is, it's very odd indeed.

EMILY. Did he say this wasn't the right place?

EDWARD. Yes. We took a wrong turning.

EMILY. What about the house? Can we go and look at it tomorrow, when the car's mended?

EDWARD. Yes, don't worry. We'll make a point of seeing it tomorrow.

EMILY. What if Mum's still worried about catching her plane to America?

EDWARD. You don't imagine, do you, that a little thing like catching a plane to America would be enough to put her off coming to see her new house?

EMILY. We don't have time to go now, do we?

EDWARD. I'm afraid not. (*Pause.*) Shall I tell you something Emily?

EMILY. What?

EDWARD. Oh, it doesn't matter.

EMILY (*stopping*). Hey look at that tree over by the gate! It's exactly like the picture of the tree you did above the mantelpiece in the living-room. The gate's in just the same place and everything. It's exactly like it.

EDWARD (*Laughs*). No it isn't. It's nothing like it at all.

EMILY. It's exactly like it if you ask me.

They walk on.

EDWARD. I think we should have invited that chap to come with us you know. He seemed such a sensible type. We could've climbed up Bredon, the three of us together, and sat on the top looking down over the fields. We could've counted how many streams there are, and you could've made us laugh by telling us the names of all the villages we could see. Not their real names, but your own, invented names. Better names. And on the way down we could've told each other stories to help pass the time.

EMILY. Stories about what?

EDWARD. Oh anything. Dead kings. Lost princesses. Vanished lands.

EMILY. Did you tell that man you've been here before?

EDWARD. Were you listening to our conversation?

EMILY. I only thought I heard you tell him, that you'd been here before.

EDWARD. You know, Emily, it's very rude to listen to people when they're trying to lie convincingly. It puts them off. However, since you ask, yes, I did tell him that, but it was only a lie, and I only told him a lie to make him happy.

EMILY. Why would telling him a lie make him happy?

EDWARD. It was probably a great relief to him to hear that we had a very specific reason for wanting to move to this area. Adults generally like to think that they know what they're doing, and that they can give reasons which will seem to explain their actions. The fact that I once used to know this area would seem to him a good reason for my wanting to come back here. He would assume that this was an area having happy associations for me, and that I wished to reawaken these associations in my mind.

EMILY. But it's not true? You didn't?

EDWARD. No.

EMILY. I don't think he looked very happy. He looked just the same to me.

EDWARD. That's because he wasn't an actor. Ordinary people never look like their feelings.

EMILY. When you were talking I saw a grave where the man and his wife were both buried in it even though they both died at different times. How do they do that, do they just dig it up again and put the other person in?

EDWARD. Yes, he does it, the man we were just speaking to.

EMILY. Euurgh, I wonder if it ever happened that he accidentally trod on the coffin underneath and his foot went right through the lid.

EDWARD. I think you'll find that they take special precautions in a case like that. The vicar will probably issue him with a pair of special ultra-lightweight boots.

EMILY. You know your wife that died before you met us, do you miss her?

EDWARD. Is this important?

EMILY. But do you?

EDWARD. No, I don't miss her. I did at first, you know. But not now.

EMILY. But do you think about her?

EDWARD. Yes.

EMILY (*as the church bells ring out*). Carol says that when you hear church bells ringing it isn't really church bells, they use a record. Is that true?

EDWARD. Probably.

EMILY. Shall we be getting back now, its (*Pause.*) hey, my watch is broken!

EDWARD. It's probably just stopped. Wind it up.

EMILY. You can't wind these up. It's broken. Stupid, horrible thing.

EDWARD. We'll get you another one, just the same. We'll go past the same garage on the way home tomorrow.

EMILY. But I want *this* one. I like *this* one. Jesus, and I only got it this morning.

EDWARD. Don't swear like that.

EMILY. Mummy does. She says it all the time. (*Pause.*) Do you think she'll be very disappointed when she finds out we didn't get to see the house?

EDWARD. I think she'll be very disappointed indeed. (*He lies down on the grass.*)

EMILY. Don't lie there!

EDWARD. Why not?

EMILY. It's on top of somebody's grave.

EDWARD. I'm sure they won't mind.

EMILY. Aren't we going back?

EDWARD. Soon. I thought we might just lie here for a minute or two and close our eyes and let the sun shine on our faces and try to fall into a state of contemplative ecstasy.

EMILY. I don't want to. (*Pause.*) Edward, I'm hungry. (*Long pause. A nightingale close by begins to sing.*) Edward.

EDWARD. Ssh, listen: it's a nightingale. A very rare sound. You hardly ever hear one nowadays.

EMILY. I hate this watch. How do you know it's a nightingale?

EDWARD (*getting up*). How do I know? Because it was on a record I borrowed once from the gramophone library. *Bird Songs of the British Isles, Volume Four*. In fact, I think it's the same damn bird, I think I recognise it. Let's go. We're late already . . .

8

Later. At the farmhouse.

PAMELA. So not only did you fail to see the house, you failed even to get to the right village.

EDWARD. I explained why to you – the end of the signpost was broken off.

PAMELA. But for chrissakes Edward, the wrong village. Didn't you have your little map with you?

EDWARD. Yes, of course I had the map with me, but that's an Act of God, they don't mark Acts of God on ordnance survey maps.

PAMELA. Mrs Whatsername kept asking where you were, and I kept saying you should be back any minute, you'd only gone four miles. I felt a complete fool.

EDWARD. Well I apologised very nicely to her. Here, I got you a newspaper.

PAMELA. The *Sunday Express*? What did you get this rag for?

EDWARD. I like it. All human life is there. It was the only one she had left in the shop.

PAMELA. I detest it. Smug, right-wing crap.

EDWARD. Anyway it was very nice of her to keep the food warm for us. (*Pause.*) What did you think of the food at the party last night?

PAMELA. I didn't. I wasn't hungry.

EDWARD. You should've tried the quiche, it was delicious.

PAMELA. I just told you, I wasn't hungry. Why can't you listen?

EDWARD (*opening the window*). They're still playing out here. (*Pause.*) I didn't indulge myself, but I think the cocaine was a particularly happy choice of ice-breaker. Smiles all round, I noticed. At one point I went to the toilet and found a chap standing fully clothed under the shower with a plate of chille in his hand. 'It's too hot,' he kept saying, 'the fire risk is incredible.' (*Pause.*) Who was the small bearded man with the bald head wearing all the necklaces and jewellery and earrings and so on? You were talking to him.

PAMELA. Richard Topham.

EDWARD. I thought Richard Topham was your dentist?

PAMELA. He is.

EDWARD. A dentist with earrings?

PAMELA. What's wrong with that?

EDWARD. There's nothing actually wrong with it. I suppose he takes them out when he's working.

PAMELA. If you were shocked by Richard, God knows what you made of Jonathan Reeves with the diamond stud in his nose.

EDWARD. Most of your friends are men, aren't they?

PAMELA. This is a man's world, sweetie. Or hadn't you noticed?

EDWARD. What does he do, that chap? He was so determined not to tell me what he did. I suppose now you'll tell me he's a solicitor.

PAMELA. He's the editor of *Open Flap*.

EDWARD. What's that, an aircraft magazine?

PAMELA. It's a girlie magazine.

EDWARD. Why does he do it, if he's so ashamed of it?

PAMELA. He's not ashamed of it. When he took that magazine over two years ago it was nowhere. Now it's the fastest growing men's magazine on the market.

EDWARD. Then why wouldn't he tell me?

PAMELA. I don't know why not. Perhaps he thought it was boring, the way you kept asking him all the time.

EDWARD. He should've just told me, I would've stopped. Anyway I was only trying to make conversation. I didn't really give a damn what he did. Why do people always feel they have to be so *interesting*?

PAMELA. Well then maybe he didn't like the *way* you were asking him. I mean, you're so bloody polite, Edward. It's rude, it embarrasses people. You should try to be a bit more spontaneous. You're too reserved.

EDWARD. I was born reserved. I'm fifty-three, Pamela. I'm too old for all that reggae or whatever it is. I felt out of place.

PAMELA. You always feel out of place, no matter where you are. It's not your age, it's you. You make no effort, you don't try,

I don't know, you . . . you don't seem to care about anything.

EDWARD. Were there many celebrities there last night? I had the strong impression of being in the presence of many celebrities. The cut of the faces seemed so familiar.

PAMELA. God you are so bitter aren't you? You can hardly swallow it.

EDWARD. Hardly swallow what?

PAMELA. Nothing.

EDWARD. Come on. Hardly swallow what?

PAMELA. Nothing. I didn't mean anything. It's just that you criticise, all the time. (*Pause.*) Edward, can we have a serious talk?

EDWARD. Fire away.

PAMELA. I mean serious.

EDWARD. I'm listening.

PAMELA. I don't think this is working out between us.

EDWARD. Please don't start all this again.

PAMELA. What do you mean, all this?

Sound effects from the cricket pitch; more applause.

EDWARD. Oh for heaven's sake there's another one gone. Run out. One short of his fifty. Skidded in his brown shoes. The village doesn't seem to be doing very well at the moment.

PAMELA. I want you to think about it. Please.

EDWARD. There's nothing to think about.

PAMELA. Look at us. We do nothing but argue all the time. We're not happy are we? This is not happiness.

EDWARD. Happiness isn't sweets, you know. If you're happy just a few times in your life then you're damn lucky, and you should get down on your knees and thank God for it, and not go around whining for more, more all the time. We're doing all right Pamela. Don't expect too much.

PAMELA. Doing all right isn't enough, damn you. I want more happiness. I will have it. We're not even lovers anymore. It's been months since you touched me.

EDWARD. So what? Have you finished with this paper? (*Taking it up.*)

PAMELA. What did you just say?

EDWARD (*reads*). 'MURDER – AND THE WEAPON WAS A PIECE

OF CHEESE.' Chap here stabbed his wife to death with a wedge of Parmesan. Othello Federici, 53-year-old restaurant owner. They found traces of cheese in the wound. God, how I detest passionate people.

PAMELA (*strikes the paper from him*). Put it down! I'm trying to talk to you.

EDWARD. Talk to me. That's all we ever do: talk talk talk. If you want to talk go to a psychoanalyst.

PAMELA. God, what has happened to you?

EDWARD. There must've been one there last night. Was it the American? I get the impression that there's quite a high incidence of Americanism among the fancy. Or is that simply an illusion created by the vocabulary? How I hated those people last night. Oh not the people, I didn't hate the people, it wasn't the people I hated – it was the life, the stupid, empty life. (*Pause.*) Oh God, things aren't going right for us at the moment, I know. You work too hard, and I'm not getting enough work. If only we could move out here. We could rest. Have some peace and quiet again. If we've got time tomorrow I'd like to show you the remains of the old church at Clun. There's a Roman pavement there. They unearthed it when they were knocking the church down. The extraordinary thing is that you can still see the designs on the tiles from two thousand years ago. The sexton at Clunton told me about it. Come on, it's not ten o'clock yet, let's go and have a drink. We'll ask the landlady to keep an eye on Emily while we're out.

9

Later. In the pub.

EDWARD (*drinks*). Ah that's better. We should be all right here, these out-of-the-way country pubs never close on time. You did want ice in it didn't you?

PAMELA. Yeah. Who's that pompous old sod in the photograph there?

EDWARD. It looks like Elgar, the composer.

PAMELA. He looks as if somebody's stuck a poker up his arse.

EDWARD. He was a very sensitive man was Elgar.

PAMELA. Yeah he looks it.

EDWARD. The landlord must be a music lover. (*He drinks.*) Have you heard Emily playing 'As With Gladness Men of Old' on her recorder?

PAMELA. Yeah. I have. Edward, I . . .

EDWARD (*quickly*). I'm a bit worried about her actually. At the moment. Do you think she's all right?

PAMELA. How do you mean?

EDWARD. She seems to get upset so easily these days. She shouts all the time. She started talking about the washing machine in the back garden this afternoon.

PAMELA. I know. She doesn't want me to get rid of it. She had a fit when I suggested we might give it away to a jumble sale.

EDWARD. Has she mentioned this business about Jesus' dog to you?

PAMELA. Jesus' what?

EDWARD. His dog. Susan Reynolds's grandmother has told them, that if they read the Bible very carefully, it says somewhere that Jesus had a dog.

PAMELA. She's kidding you. She was having you on. She's a great kidder is our Emily. She gets it from her dad – Eric was like that.

EDWARD. No, I think she meant it. She got so worried about the damn thing. She kept asking me, who would look after it when Jesus was crucified?

PAMELA. It's a trick to get them to read the Bible all the way through. Spot the dog and win a prize. What did you tell her?

EDWARD. I said probably the Virgin Mary would look after it. Or one of the disciples. Or perhaps one of his brothers was fond of dogs.

PAMELA. One of his brothers? Jesus never had any brothers.

EDWARD. He had four.

PAMELA. You're kidding. I never knew that. (*Pause.*) She got so upset about that calendar this afternoon. It's not like her.

EDWARD. I think maybe she knows something's going on in the house.

PAMELA. What do you mean?

EDWARD. She must've picked up some, some hint that we were thinking of moving house. Sometimes I think that child's psychic. She seems to pick things up out of thin air. Maybe we should've told her from the beginning.

PAMELA. I'm glad we didn't tell her. Anyway this child mysticism is nonsense. She's fallen out with Lydia, that's what it is. She and Lydia aren't speaking to each other at the moment, she told me.

'Last orders please ladies and gentlemen, your very last orders please'.

EDWARD. Do you want another?

PAMELA. No. You have one. Why is the landlord staring at me like that?

EDWARD. I don't know. Perhaps he's wondering if you're going to pick up all the little pieces of cigarette packet you've been ripping up under the table.

PAMELA. Oh. Oh I didn't notice.

EDWARD. Are you feeling all right?

PAMELA. Yes, yes I'm fine.

EDWARD (*drinks*). How did you spend the time while we were out getting lost this afternoon? Did you get the rest of that manuscript read?

PAMELA. Yes. Yes I read the rest of that.

EDWARD. Are you going to publish it?

PAMELA. Yes I think we will, I think it's rather good.

EDWARD. It looked like complete rubbish to me.

PAMELA. Oh I know *you* wouldn't like it. I wouldn't expect *you* to like it. But *I* like it. I think most people will like it. Most thick, ordinary people.

EDWARD. Oh stop being so relentlessly democratic. This is hopeless, pretending mediocre things are good, or interesting, when all it is is that they make a lot of money. It's ridiculous and dishonest. Why not admit it? Nobody cares a damn anyway.

PAMELA. All right then, since you insist, yes, we'll do it for money – so that the company can pay me a good wage so that *I* can pay the mortgage, *I* can pay the heating bills, *I* can pay the food bills, *I* can pay the electricity and the telephone, and for the bloody car when we get it mended tomorrow.

EDWARD. These authors, when you take them out to lunch or whatever, do they appear to be ashamed of themselves? Do they look furtively round the restaurant and hope no one recognises them?

PAMELA. No, quite the contrary.

EDWARD. It all seems so damn childish. Imagine your friends knowing that that's how you make your living. I think I'd rather be a tramp than do that.

PAMELA. Yeah. You never get shit on your shoes, do you? You leave that up to me. You're so damn proud of your honesty Edward, but look at you – what have you ever done?

EDWARD. I've worked. What has anybody else ever done? I'm not proud. I don't understand, that's all.

10

Later. Back at the farmhouse.

PAMELA (*entering the room*). Where's the light switch?

EDWARD. It's on the other wall.

PAMELA (*switching on*). Brr, shut the window.

EDWARD (*shutting the window*). My legs are a bit stiff from the walk this afternoon. I'm out of training. If we get the house I'm going to take up walking again, as a hobby. I used to love walking when I was younger. You're looking at me in a very strange way, what is it?

PAMELA. I'm going to bed. What time is it? (*She goes into the bedroom.*)

EDWARD. Ten to three, according to the church clock.

PAMELA. It can't be.

EDWARD. I must be getting the hands mixed up. It must be a quarter past ten.

PAMELA. God, isn't there a radiator or something in this bedroom?

EDWARD. You're not really cold, are you?

PAMELA. I'm freezing.

EDWARD. There's a radiator under the washhand-basin.

PAMELA. I'm putting it on full. Are you going to stay up and read for a bit?

EDWARD. Yes, I think I will stay up for a while.

PAMELA. Switch it off when you come to bed then, won't you? (*Getting into bed.*) God, it's like a breeze block this bed. Goodnight.

EDWARD. Goodnight.

A long pause. A page turning. A dog barks.

(*Clears his throat.*) People from the past are so quaint, aren't they? It says here that Edison thought a major use for the phonograph would be for recording the last words of the dying.

PAMELA. He should've been at the party last night; he'd've soon found out what phonographs are for. Is that still the crap about John McCormack?

EDWARD. Listen to this: (*Reads.*) 'So simple the construction, and so readily available the materials required for the phonograph, the event of sound recording, unlike photography, could have taken place two thousand years ago.'

PAMELA. It's a shame they never thought of it at the time. We could've had a live recording of the crucifixion: 'My God my God why hast thou forsaken me?' Version in dub.

EDWARD. Do you really think that's funny?

PAMELA. Not bad for off-the-cuff.

EDWARD. No I meant, do you think that's a fit subject for humour, or do we not bother to distinguish between such things anymore?

PAMELA. Are you being serious?

EDWARD. I'm asking you a question.

PAMELA. Oh read your book.

EDWARD. It's a serious question. Do you really think it would've been funny or interesting to make records of Jesus on the cross? I'm sure it would do very well, economically. But that's not quite what I'm asking.

PAMELA. All right. You want to talk about religion, let's talk about religion: I want you to lay off Emily. I want you to stop filling her head with all this stuff about Jesus and God. She's my daughter, and I don't want her growing up with the same shit I grew up with. I've told you what I think about the Church. I detest the bloody Church. It's taken me years to get over that shit.

EDWARD. I don't talk to her about the Church. The Church doesn't interest me. I just don't want her to grow up believing like every other stupid, smug, narrow-minded bugger that everything can be explained, that everything can be counted and quantified and classified and filed away. I don't want her to be ashamed of not understanding. I want her to grow up with some respect for life, I want her to grow up with a sense of the mystery at the heart of life.

PAMELA. You make it sound like a school dinner.

EDWARD. Ah my pet. So relentlessly flippant.

PAMELA. I'm serious, Edward. You're lucky, you weren't brought up religious. You think you've found bloody Treasure Island the way you go on. Well I was. I know what it's like to have the priest come round and your mum gives him your bloody dinner because she says you're not hungry, when in fact you're bloody starving. I'm finished with it, and I don't want my daughter going through it.

EDWARD. I know the appalling way you were brought up is a source of great pride to you, Pamela. Don't take everything so damn personally. (*Pause.*) I get so tired. I get tired of pretending to understand. I get tired of pretending to know what I'm talking about.

PAMELA. I'm not surprised, you do it all the bloody time.

EDWARD (*withdrawing*). You're such a clever girl, Pamela. Such a clever girl.

PAMELA. Don't read your book, Edward. (*Pause.*) Edward. (*Pause.*) I am talking to you. (*She comes into the sitting-room, knocks the book from his hand.*) I said *don't* read your bloody book when I'm in the middle of talking to you. You're like bloody Houdini you, you just disappear in the middle of a conversation. You're so proud of yourself, aren't you? You're so proud of your innocence and your sensitivity, but you don't bloody fool me. I see right through you. You're a liar. You're just another one of those liars. Healing the sick. Eyesight to the blind. Resurrection of the dead. Immaculate bloody conception which is the only kind of conception you seem to know anything about. It makes me physically ill, do you know it makes me physically ill to hear that little kid going on about Jesus and nails and blood and suffering. It's lies. Sick, morbid lies. And it's us that has to suffer, we're the ones who have to pay for your lies. You think you're the only sensitive person in the world, you and your feelings, but I know what you are, I'll tell you what you are – you're just a born-again Christian who designs wallpaper for chain stores that don't even fucking want them.

EDWARD (*hits her hard*). Shut your fucking mouth.

She knocks over a table. The lamp and the phone fall.

PAMELA. I'm sorry. I'm sorry. Don't touch me.

EDWARD. Your nose is bleeding.

PAMELA. I'm sorry, I didn't mean it. No please leave me, please leave me alone, I'm all right. I'm all right. Edward, I'm leaving you tomorrow.

EDWARD. What do you mean?

PAMELA. I'm not going to America. I'm leaving you.

EDWARD. Where are you going?

PAMELA. I have someone.

EDWARD. Who is it? Is it someone I know?

PAMELA. No, no, it isn't anyone you know. So you see, there's not much point in my looking at this house.

EDWARD. No. No I quite see that.

PAMELA (*pause*). Well say something. Aren't you going to say something?

EDWARD. I can't think of anything to say.

PAMELA. It's the only way, Edward. Look at us. There's nothing. Just nothing.

EDWARD. One shouldn't expect too much, you know.

PAMELA. Why do you say that? Please don't talk like that. Why do you talk like that? Sometimes I don't understand you at all. You've changed so much. You're so bitter and cynical, you talk as if you hate everything and everybody. You don't seem to care anymore. You don't talk to me. Even when you've got problems you just make a joke out of it. Sometimes I feel as if I've never really known you at all. You never speak about your life before we met. You have never ever ever talked about your first wife. I don't even know her name. D'you realise that? It's hopeless.

EDWARD. That's quite correct, I think too much about the past. I don't seem able to stop myself.

PAMELA. Well you might at least have tried to talk about it.

EDWARD. What's there to say? It's just the past. I don't know what to say about it.

PAMELA. But you could have tried. You could have tried. You don't even try.

EDWARD (*pause*). Well, sometimes I feel a thing rising up in me, and it makes me forget about everything. I feel as if it flies out from me, and takes a hold of some strong, unknown thing beyond. (*Pause.*) I'm not sure what to call it.

PAMELA (*pause*). What are you trying to say?

EDWARD. I don't know.

PAMELA (*pause*). Anyway it's for the best. For all of us. I can't go on like this.

EDWARD. No. I do realise that.

EMILY (*knocks on the door*). Mum. Mum.

EDWARD. You better go and see about your nose, the blood's on your gown.

PAMELA. Yes. (*Going.*) Don't say anything to her will you. Not yet. (*She goes to the bedroom and closes the door.*)

EDWARD (*opens the door onto the landing*). Mummy's gone to bed Emily, she's very tired. What is it?

EMILY. Can you turn the television down please? I can *hear* it.

EDWARD. All right sweetheart. Come in, come in.

EMILY (*entering*). The television woke me up. You had it up too loud.

EDWARD. I'm sorry about that. I've turned it off now.

EMILY. Who's knocked the table over?

EDWARD (*righting it*). I did. I banged into it when I was getting up. Does that phone still work?

EMILY. Yes. Why were they shouting?

EDWARD. I don't know. It was only an old film. We weren't really watching it.

EMILY. I had a nightmare.

EDWARD. Then come and sit here on my lap and tell me about it.

EMILY. All right. (*She sits.*) I dreamed that we were walking in that cemetery we were in. You said we had to go and take shelter and we went and sat down under a tree. It was horrible and dark and cold and wet, but you kept saying we had to stay there.

EDWARD. Then I was being extremely sensible, wasn't I?

EMILY. Yes, but it was like that under the tree. Everywhere else the sun was shining. And then there was a woman lying on the ground. She had on a white dress like the woman in that photograph you bought. She was wearing make-up, but her face was very pale, and her eyes were closed. You kept looking at her. You were smoking a cigarette and the smoke was drifting over to where she was. It was drifting all around and through her, and kind-of inside her, as though she wasn't really there. And then you said you had to go and ask her something because you said she knew about cars. And you began drifting and mingling into her, and when there was only your arm left you held the cigarette out to me and said I should have a smoke of it.

EDWARD. And did you?

EMILY. I woke up then. What time is it?

EDWARD. Go and look. You can see the church clock from that window.

EMILY (*away*). It says ten to three.

EDWARD. It can't be ten to three.

EMILY. It says ten to three.

EDWARD. Let me see. (*Joining her.*) So it does. It must've stopped.

EMILY. Maybe the vicar forgot to wind it up.

EDWARD. Yes. (*He moves away.*) He's probably gone out dancing somewhere and forgotten all about it.

EMILY (*still at the window; dog barking*). I think this dog here is lost. It's just walking up and down and barking and barking and barking. Shall we ring for the police to come and get it?

EDWARD. First thing tomorrow. If he's still there we'll call the police first thing in the morning.

EMILY. Are we still going to look at the house tomorrow? When the car's mended?

EDWARD. I'm afraid not pet.

EMILY. Oh why not?

EDWARD. We don't have time, unfortunately.

EMILY. Oh. Oh well. I didn't really think we'd go and look at it anyway.

EDWARD. Didn't you? Why not?

EMILY. Because if you think about it, in the old calendar, because this is 10 September, we aren't really here really, and none of this is really happening, is it? Not really.

EDWARD. No, I suppose it isn't, not really.

EMILY (*yawns*). I'm tired. I'm going in to Mum.

EDWARD. Don't wake her up if she's sleeping. Don't bang the door.

EMILY. No. Goodnight. (*She walks away and opens the bedroom door.*)

EDWARD. Emily.

EMILY. What?

EDWARD. Anything can make you happy, you know. A bird singing. Or seeing a woman in a garden, hanging out washing on a windy day. It doesn't always have to be an important thing.

EMILY. Why are you telling me that?

EDWARD. I thought you ought to know, really.

THE LAST OF A DYIN' RACE

by Christina Reid

**For Christina and Anna Corry
my grandmother and great-aunt**

Christina Reid was born and bred in Belfast where she still lives with
her three daughters. She left school at 15, worked in various boring
jobs, returned to school in her mid-thirties and subsequently studied
English, Russian Studies and Sociology at Queen's University,
Belfast, for one year before *Tea in a China Cup* won her a Thames TV
Award and a residency at the Lyric Theatre, Belfast, in 1983–4.
Paines Plough produced a rehearsed reading of *Dissenting Adults* at
the Royal Court Theatre in 1985 and then commissioned *Joyriders* for
their 1986 spring tour. Her first play *Did You Hear the One About the
Irishman?* won the UTV Drama Award in 1980. The stage version was
performed by the Royal Shakespeare Company in New York and
Washington in 1985. *The Last of a Dyin' Race* is her first radio play
and was commissioned by BBC Northern Ireland. A television
version has now been made by UTV for Channel 4. She has also had
short stories and articles published and broadcast, and is currently
working on a commissioned play for the Tricycle Theatre, London.

The Last of a Dyin' Race was first broadcast on BBC Radio 4 on
14 January 1986. The cast was as follows:

SARAH	Leila Webster
AGNES	Sheila McGibben
JOHNNIE	Peter Adair
MADGE	Maureen Dow
DAVE	Peter Quigley
FLORENCE	Heidi Reid
OLD FEMALE MOURNER	Catherine Gibson
OLD MALE MOURNER	Michael Duffy
SERGEANT	Brian Hogg
CONSTABLE PATTERSON	Peter Quigley
UNDERTAKER	David Coyle
JOE	Derek Halligan
SHARON	Frances Quinn
YOUNGER FEMALE MOURNER	Olivia Nash

Director: Susan Hogg
Running time, as broadcast: 55 minutes, 45 seconds

A music-box playing 'Au clair de la lune'. Crossfade with the sounds of a milk lorry stopping. Milk bottles being set on a step. A man whistling. Outdoor acoustic. Crossfade to indoor acoustic. The following voices are interspersed with LIZZIE McCULLOUGH's *shallow breathing.*

LIZZIE. If you don't get the milk in quick, the cats get at it.

NEIGHBOUR 1. Aye, or them bluetits.

NEIGHBOUR 2. Beaks like pneumatic drills they have . . .

LIZZIE. He brings me my tea to bed every morning.

NEIGHBOUR 1. You're a lucky woman Lizzie, not many men like Willie McCullough in half a dozen.

The music-box playing 'Au clair de la lune'.

WILLIE. Come on Lizzie girl, up ye get.

LIZZIE. Willie?

NEIGHBOUR 2. Aye, a good man, you'll miss him now he's gone . . . miss him now he's gone . . . .

WILLIE. Come on now, you'll be late for work.

LIZZIE. Willie?

NEIGHBOUR 1. She's an awful bad colour isn't she?

NEIGHBOUR 2. I knew there was somethin' wrong when I saw her milk still sittin' on the step . . . .

The music-box.

WILLIE. Drink your tea, it'll get cold . . . .

NEIGHBOUR 1. It's all right now Lizzie, your Joe's here, him and Sharon . . . .

LIZZIE mutters.

What love?

The music-box surges.

WILLIE. Come on love, up ye get . . . .

SHARON. What's she sayin' Joe?

JOE. Can't make it out Sharon, somethin' about a box . . . .

AMBULANCE MAN. No panic now missus. You'll soon be in the hospital. . . . We'll have ye right as rain in no time.

The music-box surges.

WILLIE. Come on, come on.

SHARON. What box? Make sure you lock that door Joe, she'll have money hid.

The music-box surges with LIZZIE's breathing.

WILLIE. Up ye get girl, come on.

Crossfade to SARAH washing dishes; indoor acoustic, small kitchen. DAVE calls from the next room.

DAVE. Hey Mammy!

SARAH. What?

DAVE. Are there any more spuds?

The sound of water running out of the sink.

SARAH. No there aren't. I declare to God, Dave, feeding you is like feeding the five thousand.

During SARAH's last words we crossfade with her from the kitchen to the sitting-room – we hear a rattle of a plate against the hearth.

SARAH. What do you think you're doing?

DAVE. Nothin'.

SARAH. Nothin' . . . you were stealing a spud off your da's plate, so you were . . . ach Dave. You've got gravy all over the hearth now.

DAVE. Sorry.

SARAH. So you should be, stealing your father's dinner. You'd as much on your own plate as would have satisfied two men and a wee lad.

Sounds of SARAH cleaning up the hearth.

DAVE. Mammy?

SARAH. What?

DAVE. Can I ask you something?

SARAH. What?

DAVE. Every Saturday, as long as I can remember, you've been makin' the dinner at five o'clock on the dot . . . .

SARAH. Aye.

DAVE. And every Saturday my da doesn't come home from the pub till six o'clock, and you put his dinner between two plates beside the fire to keep it warm. . . .

SARAH. Aye.

DAVE. And by the time he eats it, it's like a burnt offerin' . . . .

SARAH. It's his own fault, he knows we have our dinner at five.

DAVE. Well, would you never think of havin' the dinner at six?

SARAH. We always have our Saturday dinner at five.

DAVE. Why?

SARAH. Because that's Saturday dinner-time, that's why . . . and anyway, if I started makin' it at six o'clock Johnnie Maguire would soon catch on and start comin' home at seven o'clock. Your da always comes home late for his dinner on a Saturday, so he does. My da was just the same.

DAVE sighs resignedly and continues eating. The door opens and JOHNNIE MAGUIRE rushes in.

JOHNNIE. Sarah.

SARAH. What are you doin' home at this time on a Saturday, Johnnie?

DAVE. Have they closed all the pubs or what, Da?

JOHNNIE. Listen Sarah, I'm on my way from the match to the pub, and who do you think I spy comin' in the top of our street?

SARAH. Who?

JOHNNIE. Big Agnes Drumm, that's who, and she's carryin' her black beg. Somebody must be dead, Sarah.

SARAH. Your oul head's away. If there was anybody dead around here, I'd be the first to know about it . . . .

JOHNNIE. I'm tellin' ye . . . .

SARAH. And anyway, what would she be carrying the black beg for? It's thirty years and more since Agnes Drumm washed and laid out the dead. The undertakers do all that nigh.

There is a loud knock on the door.

Dave, look out the window see who that is.

DAVE. It's a big woman in a black coat . . . and she's carrying a black beg.

JOHNNIE (*nervously*). I told ye Sarah.

DAVE. Do we all hide, or will I let her in?

SARAH. You just sit down and behave yourself. I'll let Agnes in.
(*Receding.*)

The front door opens, off – distant street noise.

Come in and sit yourself down, Agnes.

AGNES (*approaching*). Much obliged, Sarah. Afternoon, Mr Maguire.
I hope you're keepin' well.

JOHNNIE. Very well, Mrs Drumm . . . very very well . . . never felt
better in my life . . . I'll just have my dinner while it's warm if
that's all right with you.

He takes the plate off the hearth and sits. Sounds of JOHNNIE *and*
DAVE *eating throughout the following.*

SARAH. You're not lookin' yourself Agnes . . . is something wrong?

AGNES. Our Lizzie's gone.

SARAH. Ach Agnes, when?

AGNES. This mornin'. She was took bad sudden, and was rushed
into the Royal Victoria, but she only lasted a couple of hours.

JOHNNIE. Sorry for your trouble, Mrs Drumm.

AGNES. Much obliged Mr Maguire.

SARAH. I'm real sorry, Agnes. I'll get the linen out and we'll
go over.

AGNES. You needn't bother Sarah, she's not comin' home.

SARAH. What do you mean, she's not comin' home?

AGNES. What I say. Our Joe, may God forgive him, is not bringin'
his mother back til her own house.

JOHNNIE. He can't leave her lyin' up in the hospital . . . .

AGNES. She's lyin' in Charlie Wilson's funeral parlour, that's where
she's lyin' . . . all by herself in Charlie Wilson's funeral parlour.

SARAH. Dave! Get Mrs Drumm a glass of whiskey. It's in the
left hand cupboard above the cooker, behind the cough linctus.
Move yourself.

DAVE. OK, OK. (*Receding.*)

SARAH. Agnes, Joe would never do the like of that til his
own mother.

AGNES. It's not Joe's doin'. Joe does what he's told. It's that Sharon
one. I don't know what our Joe ever saw in her, she always was a
disturber, she could cause an argument between two breast bones
that one.

Distant sounds of DAVE *searching for the bottle, finding it, pouring it.*

JOHNNIE. You're Lizzie's sister, Mrs Drumm, could you not stop them?

AGNES. I'm only her half-sister. Joe's her son. I've no say.

DAVE (*on approach*). Here's your whiskey Mrs Drumm.

AGNES. Thank you. (*She drains the glass in one go; puts the glass on the table.*) That was grand, much obliged, son.

DAVE. Would you like another one?

AGNES. No, not just at the moment, thank you all the same.

SARAH. Are you sure you haven't got it wrong, Agnes?

AGNES. Oh no. That Sharon came round to tell me, said Joe was away makin' the arrangements. Hadn't the nerve to show his face.

SARAH. Maybe you misunderstood, Agnes. Maybe Charlie Wilson's just comin' to the house to lay Lizzie out.

AGNES. No, I've seen her. As soon as Sharon left, I got my black beg, and I went round to Charlie Wilson's personal. I thought maybe I could talk him intil lettin' me wash her and put on her good frock . . . but she was already done by the time I got there.

JOHNNIE. It's a quare while since you laid anybody out, Mrs Drumm . . . .

SARAH. Eat your dinner, Johnnie.

JOHNNIE. I'm only sayin' . . . .

SARAH. You were always the best so ye were, Agnes.

AGNES. I know it's not the fashion nomore . . . times change . . . but I always promised our Lizzie that if God spared me, no stranger would handle her.

DAVE *sniggers.*

JOHNNIE. Is there no puddin' the day, Sarah?

SARAH. Excuse me a minute, Agnes. (SARAH *gets up.*) Dave, come into the kitchen. I want a word with you! (*Receding.*)

The scrape of a chair as DAVE gets up and goes into the kitchen.

DAVE. OK, OK.

Crossfade from the sitting-room to the kitchen. The door is closed.

SARAH. Will you stop sittin' there grinnin' all over your face. Mrs Drumm is very upset so she is, and so am I. Shift yourself and give me down that tin.

DAVE. Well, it's all daft.

The sound of a tin on the draining-board. A drawer is opened. The sound of cutlery while SARAH searches.

What's wrong with funeral parlours anyway?

SARAH. Nobody from round here was ever buried from a funeral parlour. It's just not done.

DAVE. You're just put-out 'cause you can't get usin' the death linen.

The drawer slams shut.

SARAH. Listen you, when anybody round here dies, they're laid out in their own bedroom, and I set up the room nice with starched white linen over the mirrors and the furniture and the bed.

DAVE. It's creepy!

SARAH *attacks the tin with the tin-opener.*

SARAH. It's an honour. My grandmother, God rest her, was entrusted with it in the first place because she could be relied on to keep it in good order and not pawn it, no matter how hard times were.

DAVE. I still say it's creepy, and so are dead bodies lyin' for inspection in open coffins!

SARAH. It's a mark of respect. You lie for three days and all your family and friends come to see ye.

DAVE. It's weird.

SARAH. It's tradition.

DAVE. She's dead, she won't know anything about it.

SARAH. It's her right! You young ones are all the same.

SARAH *takes down a bowl and pours the peaches into it.*

I suppose when I go it'll be as quick as ye can get me out of your road intil one of them places . . . .here, take them peaches intil your da before the hunger kills him.

DAVE. Am I not gettin' any?

SARAH *takes another small tin of peaches out of the cupboard and thumps it down.*

SARAH. Here, help yourself. By God, you and your da'll not die for the want of good food, that's for sure.

Crossfade to another room. We are in LIZZIE's house. We hear someone shuffling through a box of photos – silence – a sigh.

SHARON (*from a distance*). Joe! Where are you?

JOE. I'm here Sharon.

A door opens – SHARON enters.

SHARON. What were you doing?

JOE. I found a box of photos, I was just looking through them.

SHARON. Oh aye, you just relax and look at photos while I do all the work. I don't know why I'm bothering anyway, packing up all this oul rubbish. We'll be lucky if we get a tenner for it down in the market. Still, you never know. Some old ornaments are worth a fortune these days. You see that vase . . . is it ruby glass do you think?

JOE. I wouldn't know, Sharon.

SHARON. Well, is it old? Was it here when you were a child?

JOE. Oh, it has always sat there. I think it belonged to my father's mother.

SHARON. Don't you touch it. I'll pack that away myself. You get on with the rest of the stuff down here while I'm up the stairs. And don't be breaking nothing. (*She recedes.*)

A door bangs. Cut back to SARAH's *house.*

AGNES. I haven't told you the worst of it yet, Sarah . . . they're havin' her . . . cremated . . . .

SARAH. They're what?

JOHNNIE. Away to hell!

AGNES. First thing Monday morning.

SARAH. You mean they're not even givin' poor Lizzie the proper three days lyin' out?

AGNES. They can't get rid of her quick enough.

JOHNNIE. It's a bad do, that.

SARAH. Right Agnes, let's go.

The scrape of a chair as SARAH *gets up.*

AGNES. There's nuthin' we can do Sarah, Joe's her next of kin.

SARAH. And we're her friends and relations . . . we're entitled to pay our respects, us and everybody what knew her . . . and that includes you two.

DAVE. Count me out.

SARAH. Be down at Charlie Wilson's funeral parlour before the pubs close, or I'll know the reason why. (*Receding.*)

The door slams.

DAVE. What was all that about?

JOHNNIE. Your mother's got the light of battle in her eye . . . poor oul Lizzie . . . imagine . . . a funeral parlour . . . and cremation . . . it doesn't bear thinkin' about . . . .

DAVE. Ach Da! You don't agree with all this oul nonsense do you?

JOHNNIE. There's a lot to be said for the old ways. Like your granda used to say . . . no matter how hard your life was, you could always rely on the neighbours to give you a good send-off when you were dead. Man, I could tell you a tale or two about some of the wakes I've been at in my time.

DAVE. I'm away to the pub.

JOHNNIE. The very thing. We'll have a few bevvies you and me, and we'll get a wee carry-out for the funeral parlour.

DAVE. My ma'll kill ye!

JOHNNIE. Not at all, sure you can't have a wake without a wee drop of the hard stuff.

Crossfade to the funeral parlour. Funeral music is playing. CHARLIE WILSON *hums along with it. He is drinking tea. A door opens off with an old-fashioned shop bell on it.* CHARLIE *quickly turns off the music and gets up.* SARAH, MADGE, AGNES *and* FLORENCE *enter.*

SARAH. Good evening, Mr Wilson.

UNDERTAKER. Can I be of any assistance?

AGNES. About Lizzie McCullough . . . .

UNDERTAKER. Oh yes, it's Mrs Drumm, isn't it?

AGNES. That's correct. And this is Sarah.

SARAH. Good evening.

AGNES. And Madge, and Madge's daughter, Florence.

MADGE. ⎫
FLORENCE. ⎭ Hello.

AGNES. We've come to set up our Lizzie proper.

UNDERTAKER. I beg your pardon?

AGNES. Granted. Right girls, she's in here . . . .

The sound of a heavy curtain being drawn back.

UNDERTAKER. Excuse me! Eh . . . ladies?

Crossfade to the coffin.

AGNES. Well, Sarah, there she is. Lyin' in this place all by herself and not a one guardin' her.

SARAH. Not any more Agnes. There's you and me.

MADGE. And there's me and my Florence.

AGNES. Isn't it awful bare? Not as much as a single flower.

SARAH. Well there is now Agnes. I'll say this much for you and your Florence, Madge, yous make a beautiful wreath, the pair of you.

FLORENCE. Where'll I put the wreath, Mammy?

UNDERTAKER. There's a hook on the wall . . . above the coffin . . . eh . . . we make wreaths here you know . . . .

AGNES. I don't see much sign of it . . . .

UNDERTAKER. Oh we usually keep them intil the day of the funeral . . . so that they're fresh you know . . . .

AGNES. Fresh for who?

UNDERTAKER. For the funeral . . . the graveside . . . .

AGNES. She's bein' cremated. her ashes are to be scattered in a Garden of Remembrance, whatever that might be.

SARAH. I assume we'll have full use of the big room.

UNDERTAKER. I'm sorry, I don't quite follow . . . .

SARAH. The big room what leads into this wee room . . . .

UNDERTAKER. Oh, I see you're going to have a small service the day of the funeral . . . .

AGNES. That's to take place at the crematorium. She means for now . . . .

UNDERTAKER. What exactly are you planning . . . ?

SARAH. I'll just drape the white linen over the lectern and the table, would you like that, Agnes?

AGNES. That would be very nice, Sarah.

UNDERTAKER. Linen?

During the following, SARAH *shakes out the sheets and drapes them over the furniture.*

SARAH. Normally these would be for coverin' Lizzie's bedroom suite, but under the circumstances, this'll hafta do. At least when the people come, they'll see it's all bein' done right and proper.

UNDERTAKER. Are there many more people coming?

SARAH. Why? Do you close at a certain hour, like the pubs?

UNDERTAKER. Oh dear me, no. We provide a 24-hour service.

SARAH. I'm glad to hear it.

UNDERTAKER. Would you like the music?

AGNES. What music?

UNDERTAKER. We have music taped. You just press that switch beside the coffin.

AGNES. Now that might be nice, Lizzie always loved a good tune.

FLORENCE. Can I switch it on?

UNDERTAKER. Yes, yes of course Miss . . . .

FLORENCE. Florence.

UNDERTAKER. Florence . . . .

The same music as at the beginning of the scene.

AGNES. It's a bit doleful isn't it? Do you not have somethin' a bit
more cheerful?

UNDERTAKER. It's Handel.

SARAH. Is that a fact?

AGNES. Turn that off, Florence. It would make ye weep.

MADGE. Aye love, turn it off. That would really depress ye,
so it would.

The music is turned off.

SARAH. Well now, this wee room doesn't look so bad with the linen
set out, takes the bare look off it doesn't it?

AGNES. Aye. But them fluorescent lights is awful cold.

UNDERTAKER. Would you like me to switch one of them off?

AGNES. Do you not have a nice wee lamp or nuthin'?

MADGE. I'll bring one down later, Mrs Drumm.

AGNES. Thanks very much love. I'm much obliged.

SARAH. Do you have cups and plates here Mr Wilson?

UNDERTAKER. Cups and plates?

SARAH. No, I didn't think so. Just as well we brought our own.
What's in there, through that door?

UNDERTAKER. Oh, just a small sink, and a camping stove. It's
where I make myself a cup of tea after dealing with those
bereaved during the night . . . .

SARAH. That'll do rightly. Madge! Bring the food in here!

A door opens.
The sound of bags being picked up and carried through.

UNDERTAKER. Food? Ladies . . . I must . . . .

SARAH (*off*). Now don't worry, Mr Wilson. We have everything
under control. If we need anything else we'll let you know . . . .
(*She approaches.*) Oh, by the way, do you have any more chairs?

UNDERTAKER. More chairs?

SARAH. Aye, what's here'll never seat all Lizzie's friends.

Crossfade to LIZZIE's *house. We are with* SHARON *in the bedroom.*

SHARON. Joe! Bring me up a couple of them black sacks! These oul
clothes are fit fer nuthin' but the ragman.

The sound of coins rattling inside a box.

What's this?

JOE. Here's the sacks, Sharon.

The sound of plastic sacks being put down.

SHARON. There's somethin' rattlin' in this oul box.

She rattles it.

How do ye open it?

JOE. You push that wee knob at the side.

The box springs open.

SHARON. It's foreign money.

JOE. It all come along with my father's stuff, after the war.

The sound of the music-box playing 'Au clair de la lune'.

SHARON. It's a music-box.

JOE. He bought it in France. It was to be for her birthday. Only he never got to give it to her . . . you know it hasn't played in years. I broke it when I was a wee lad. She nearly killed me.

The sound of the lid shutting. The music stops.

SHARON. I don't like music-boxes. They're creepy. Here (*She hands him the box. It rattles.*) put it with the ruby glass, you never know, it might be worth a bob or two, an' even if it's not, the coins'll be worth the face value anyway.

SHARON *begins to busily fill the sacks with old clothes.*

JOE. A wee bit of my father . . . .

SHARON. What? (SHARON *stops.*)

JOE. A wee bit of my father . . . it's what she called the French money. It was in his pocket when he got killed, you know.

SHARON *starts to fill the sacks even more energetically.*

SHARON. No I don't know, and I don't want to know. We're here to clear the house, not to reminisce about World War II. Your Aunt Agnes'll do enough of that for all of us.

Crossfade to sounds of a large crowd gathering in the funeral parlour. A hum of conversation punctuated with people saying 'Sorry for your trouble, Mrs Drumm' and AGNES replying 'Much obliged'. Then the conversations become audible. Focus in on:

MOURNER 1. Lizzie didn't suffer or nuthin' did she, Mrs Drumm?

AGNES. I wasn't there. Our Joe never thought fit to let me know that my only sister was dyin'.

MOURNER 1. That's shockin'.

SARAH. Here Agnes. Have a wee sandwich, you haven't had a bite this day.

AGNES (*feigning reluctance*). I don't think I could stomach anything.

SARAH. Now, Agnes, you owe it to Lizzie to keep your strength up.

FLORENCE. Ah, go on, Mrs Drumm, there's roast beef and cooked ham. Take two, they're awful small.

AGNES. Well all right then.

> AGNES *takes sandwiches and eats throughout the following.*

And maybe I'll just have one of them buns while I'm at it. Much obliged, Florence.

FLORENCE. I'll just take them round.

> AGNES *eats.*

AGNES. Nice wee girl that, isn't she?

SARAH. Aye indeed, I wish I'd brought my slippers. These oul shoes are cuttin' the feet off me.

AGNES. Lovely buns them, Sarah, very tasty. Our Lizzie always loved an iced fancy when things were gettin' her down.

SARAH. Aye, she hadn't an easy life, God help her.

AGNES. She was only eight when her mother died, you know.

SARAH. Aye, and she wasn't more than ten or eleven when your mother died givin' birth to you, Agnes.

MOURNER 1. Imagine that, your father was very unfortunate, Mrs Drumm.

AGNES. My father was an oul bugger . . . drove two good women to an early grave. Lizzie had no childhood worth talkin' about, what with takin' care of me and tryin' to keep my da sober.

> *A cup and saucer rattling.*

I wouldn't mind my tea toppin' up if you've a minute, Sarah, them buns are nice, but they're awful dry in the middle.

> *Keep background level the same but crossfade speech to focus on a separate group talking in another part of the room. Throughout these scenes at the funeral parlour, the guests are eating and drinking.*

MOURNER 2 (*old man*). The da died when Lizzie was about eighteen, fell down the steps of Rinty's bar and broke his neck. Only good turn he ever done Lizzie in his life.

MADGE. Imagine that.

MOURNER 3 (*old woman*). Do you remember the night thon widow man from up the road asked Lizzie to marry him?

MOURNER 2. Do I what? It was the best bit of sport in the street since the night of Hugie McArdle's wake, when they propped him up in the coffin with a bottle of stout in his hand so that he could join the celebrations.

MOURNER 3. The widow man came runnin' out of Lizzie's house like a scalded cat, and her after him, beatin' him about the head with the fire tongs.

MOURNER 2. 'Ye skittery ghost,' she shouted, 'come and live with you and put our Agnes in a home? Away back to the midden ye came from!'

MOURNER 3. Man it was the best night's crack.

MADGE. Did you hear that Joe's havin' her cremated?

MOURNER 3. I never did agree with the like of that.

MOURNER 2. Me neither, I think that's takin' ashes to ashes a bit too far myself.

Crossfade to a different group.

SARAH. God help Agnes now she has nobody.

MOURNER 1. Is Mrs Drumm's husband dead?

SARAH. Not at all. He ran off to England with a money-lender from the top of the road, donkey's years ago. Carmen Miranda Robinson her name was. Her mother was a great picturegoer.

MOURNER 1. And was she married too?

SARAH. Oh aye, she was married to the Co-op insurance man, Johnnie Robinson his name was.

MOURNER 1. Was that the Johnnie Robinson that kept the tame monkey in the back yard until the cruelty stepped in and put a stop til it?

SARAH. No, that was Jimmy Robinson. Johnnie Robinson dyed his hair ginger, wore a hard hat when he was collectin' the insurance money.

MOURNER 1. Whatever become of Jimmy Robinson?

SARAH. Ach he took to the drink. Never was the same after they took the oul monkey away from him.

Crossfade to a different group.

MADGE. All the same, it's a funny sort of job for a woman . . . layin' out the dead . . . .

MOURNER 2. Oh, the weemin always done it.

MOURNER 3. The men were too afeard.

MADGE. And yet, now it's all men who do the undertakin'.

MOURNER 3. Aye, and men who bring the childer into the world as well.

MOURNER 2. The world's gone mad, so it has . . . men doin' weemin's work.

MADGE. What exactly did she do . . . Mrs Drumm . . . I mean . . . what does she carry in that black beg?

MOURNER 3. Nobody knows for sure . . . secret of the trade . . . .

MOURNER 2. It was always a big strappin' woman done it. The one before Mrs Drumm was built like a Mullingar heifer.

MOURNER 3. Well, they had to be, didn't they? You know what it's like yourself Madge, puttin' a nappy on a strugglin' infant, imagine havin' to do the same for a big workin' man and him a dead weight. They put a plastic contraption on your private parts in the 'ospitals nigh, before you're even gone. I had a wee geek under the sheets when my cousin Stanley was in the coma.

MADGE (*shuddering*). God, money wouldn't pay ye would it?

MOURNER 2. Mrs Drumm was always very understandin' as far as the payment was concerned. Them as had it slipped her a few shillins and them as hadn't gave her a sup of whiskey . . . she always drunk it neat, like a man.

MOURNER 3. Nigh Lizzie, she was always very partial to a wee sherry or a drop of port.

Crossfade to the pub. Background music. Much less chatter than at the wake.

JOHNNIE. Do ye know what must be the worst thing about bein' a corpse?

DAVE. What's that, Da?

JOHNNIE. Not bein' able to join in the drinkin' at yer own wake.

DAVE. Very good, Da.

JOHNNIE. I'm serious. Lyin' there an' everybody round ye havin' a whale of a time. You see the night oul Hughie McArdle died? They propped him up in the coffin with a bottle of stout in his hand. I swear to God he was smilin'.

DAVE. It's called rigor mortis, Da.

JOHNNIE. Course, Hughie died smilin'. He was over there, sittin' at that bar, and he just keeled over. Went out like a light, so he did.

DAVE. It's your turn to get them in, Da.

JOHNNIE. No, it's time we were on our way.

DAVE. What are ye talkin' about? It's only gone half ten.

JOHNNIE. We have to go an' pay our respects to Lizzie. I promised yer mother.

DAVE. Yer always promisin' my mother.

JOHNNIE. This is different . . . . have ye any readies?

DAVE. I've about a fiver. Why?

JOHNNIE. We'll hafta have a whip round.

DAVE. What are ye talkin' about?

JOHNNIE. The weemin are good at organisin' the food an' the flowers, but they can't be relied on for the liquid refreshment. I suppose it comes of runnin' the house all the time. (*He shouts:*) Hey, Alec, Charlie! A wee word if ye please . . . .

Crossfade back to funeral parlour.

MOURNER 3. I wonder who'll get Lizzie's house?

MADGE. I heard that the rentman's sellin' them all off.

MOURNER 3. I told our Kathleen's youngest to get in quick. You never know, she might get it cheap, it needs a lot doing to it.

MOURNER 2. That oul rentman never sells anything cheap.

MADGE (*receding*). I'll just go and see if our Florence wants a hand with the tea.

(*Close.*) Listen Florence, as soon as we get home the night, remind me to phone our Marion to warn her than them Carsons is after Lizzie's house.

FLORENCE. Our Marion wouldn't live in that oul house, sure it's dunderin' in.

MADGE. If her and Alec get in quick, they might get it fer next to nuthin' and then they could apply for one of them housin' executive grants. I believe you can get up to three thousand . . . sure you couldn't beat it, it's like money from America.

Crossfade to the corpse. It's much quieter in here. The wake is distant.

SARAH. Are you all right, Agnes?

AGNES. I was just tellin' Lizzie there'll be hordes of them after her house, first thing Monday mornin'.

SARAH. Now Agnes, you don't want to be standin' in here, thinkin' long and upsettin' yourself.

AGNES (*to* LIZZIE). Ach Lizzie love, you and Willie McCullough done the house up lovely the two of yous, and then he went and got himself killed the week before the end of the war, and you seven months gone. You didn't call Joe after him in case it brought bad luck . . . but he was the one brought you bad luck. (*To* SARAH:) No sign of him and that Sharon yet?

SARAH. They'll probably not appear till the day of the funeral.

AGNES. She'll be here. Look, Charlie Wilson has forgot to take Lizzie's weddin' ring off, and Sharon won't be lettin' a bit of valuable old gold go up in smoke in the crematorium.

SARAH. Lizzie always said she wanted to be buried with her weddin'
ring on.

AGNES. But she's not being buried is she? No Sarah, I won't have
that Sharon one wearin' it. It's not right. Give me your hand
Lizzie, love.

The rustle of linen – AGNES *takes the ring off.*

There now. I'll take care of this for you, I promise.

SARAH. Sharon'll be askin' for that.

AGNES. She can ask, but she'll not get.

SARAH. What if Joe wants to wear it?

AGNES. Over my dead body! I promise ye this much, Lizzie, I'll see
that your ashes are buried fernenst Willie, and I'll drop this in
alongside ye.

Crossfade to LIZZIE's *house.*

SHARON. Joe! Will you move yourself or we'll be here all night!
Stop moonin' around lookin' at things . . . . What's that yer
clutchin'?

JOE. It's a photo of my father in his army uniform.

SHARON. Let us see? God, she didn't marry him fer his looks
did she?

JOE. She said he was very gentle-spoken . . . .

SHARON. Here, that's something we haven't come across . . .
yer da's medal. Maybe it's in the box with the coins. Have a look
and see.

JOE. My mother said the whole road turned out for his funeral.
(*Moving off.*)

SHARON. Your mother lived in the past. They all do around here.

Sounds of the music-box. Then glass breaking.

SHARON. Ach fer God's sake, Joe. I warned you to be careful of
that ruby glass!

JOE. I never touched it . . . .

SHARON. Broke itself did it?

JOE. Honest, I was nowhere near it. It just shattered.

SHARON. Will you turn that thing off! Close the lid.

JOE. The lid is closed, Sharon . . . . It won't stop . . . .

Swell the music, cut back into the funeral parlour.

MADGE. Lizzie was nearly 40 when she married Willie McCullough.

MOURNER 1. You'd wonder why she bothered at that age.

MADGE. I suppose she was lonely after Agnes got married, and anyway it was wartime, a lot of people got married then.

MOURNER 1. Maybe she didn't want to die wonderin'.

They giggle at this and then stop. SARAH *returns with* AGNES.

MADGE. Ssh! She's comin' over. (*Close.*) I was just sayin', Mrs Drumm your Lizzie had Joe late in life.

AGNES (*approaching*). It was a terrible birth, nearly killed her.

SARAH. I was 36 when our Dave was born. I know it nearly killed me.

MADGE. They say it gets easier every time, but it does not.

MOURNER 1. It'll be some man said that.

SARAH. Sure your bones are bound to settle as you get older.

FLORENCE (approaching). Would you like another bun, Mrs Drumm?

AGNES. Thanks Florence, don't mind if I do.

She takes the bun off the plate and begins to eat.

FLORENCE. I'd better make some more sandwiches.

AGNES. All the same, Madge, she's a credit to you that wain. Many a young one wouldn't be bothered. They've no time for the old customs.

SARAH. Excuse me Agnes, there's our Dave . . . Dave!

DAVE (*slightly drunk*). Would you look at this lot. The last of a dyin' race.

SARAH. We'll have none of your smart remarks the night, thank you very much. Where the hell's your father?

DAVE. He's comin'.

SARAH. So's Christmas. By God I'll give it to him when I get the houl of him.

DAVE. I'm tellin' you he's on his way. I was sent ahead to tell you he's bringin' a couple of mates, so will you make some extra sandwiches.

SARAH. I'll extra sandwiches him.

Crossfade to the vestibule. The wake distant. The door opens, distant traffic. There is the rattle of bottles as JOHNNIE *and his mates come in carrying crates of alcohol. The door closes.*

UNDERTAKER. Eh, good evening gentlemen, can I help you?

JOHNNIE. You could indeed, your honour. You could take houl of this crate of Guinness. My back's broke carrying them up the road.

SARAH (*approaching*). Johnnie, and about time too.

JOHNNIE. This is a poor do, seein' Lizzie off with cups of tea. We come bringin' good cheer, don't we lads? And you needn't look like that, Sarah, we haven't forgot the ladies. One bottle of malt whiskey, one bottle of port.

He bangs them down on the table.

JOHNNIE. That'll liven your tea up.

UNDERTAKER. It's not normal practice . . . I mean this isn't quite usual . . . in a funeral parlour . . . .

Another bottle taken from the crate and banged on the table.

JOHNNIE. Here, have a bottle of stout, it'll put a bit of colour in your cheeks, son.

Crossfade to the other room – chatter – JOHNNIE distant – talking to the general assembly.

You do the honours, Dave, I'll just go and pay my respects to Lizzie. (*going off.*)

SARAH (*close*). I should be real angry with your father . . . .

DAVE. But you're not, are you?

SARAH. No, I'm not, but don't be tellin' him that. Dear God, wouldn't Lizzie have enjoyed this . . . she loved a good party. Are you not goin' in to see her?

DAVE. I am not!

SARAH. You're not afraid of an oul dead woman are ye, a big lad like you? Well, sit yourself down, son, and I'll get you a wee sandwich.

DAVE. I'm not stayin' long!

FLORENCE. Would you like a cream bun?

DAVE. Well, not very long . . . . Hello love, would *you* like a wee hand with that tray?

FLORENCE. If you like.

DAVE. My pleasure, darlin'.

Crossfade to another group.

JOHNNIE. There, that'll do you more good than tea.

MOURNER 3. Man, I was glad to see you comin' in that door, Johnnie. I was only ever at one dry wake in my life and the memory has never left me.

MOURNER 2. Do you remember the night of your granda's funeral, Johnnie?

JOHNNIE. The whiskey flowed like water.

MOURNER 3. And the banshee howled for a strucken hour.

JOHNNIE. Banshee my arse. It was our oul dog Cora howlin' to get

out. We'd locked her in the back yard because she was in heat.
My da went out and gave her a boul of stout laced with whiskey.
That soon subdued the want in her, I can tell ye.

MOURNER 2. This is a very subdued sort of a do here the night.
Lizzie always liked a bit of a singsong at a wake.

MOURNER 3. I mind Lizzie standin' up to her ankles in water in the
spinnin' mill, singin' her heart out.

JOHNNIE (*sings*).
Oh, you always know a doffer when she comes into town,
With her long yellow hair and her ringlets hangin' down,
With her rubber tied before her, and her picker in her hand,
Oh, you always know a doffer for she always gets her man,
For she always gets her man, always gets her man.
Oh, you always know a doffer, for she always gets her man.

MOURNER 3 (*sings*).
Oh, you always know a teacher when she comes into town,
With her bustle stuck behind her and on her face a frown,
And the children stand around her and her cane right in her hand,
Oh, you always know a teacher for she never gets a man,
For she never gets a man, never gets a man.
Oh, you always know a teacher, for she never gets a man.

*Everyone joins in, singing and clapping. Crossfade to the vestibule, the
singing in the background. The door opens. Traffic noises.*

SHARON. What's goin' on here!

The door closes.

UNDERTAKER. Oh dear . . . Mr and Mrs McCullough . . . good
evening . . . your mother had a lot of friends, Mr McCullough,
oh dear . . . .

SHARON. What is going on? (*She moves off.*)

JOE. Sharon.

Crossfade back into the wake.

JOHNNIE (*sings*).
Oh, you always know a doffer, when she comes into town,
With her long greasy hair and her knickers hangin' down,
And her knickers hangin' down and her knickers hangin' down,
Oh, you always know a doffer, when she comes into town,
When she comes into town.

*Clapping, shouting, etc. The cheering and singing subside as the mourners
become aware that* JOE *and* SHARON *have come in. There are whispers
of 'It's Joe and Sharon', then an uneasy silence punctuated by a few
nervous coughs.*

AGNES. Well, if it isn't the prodigal son . . . . On behalf of my dear
departed sister Elizabeth McCullough may I thank you for comin'
to pay your respects.

JOE. Aunt Agnes . . . .

AGNES. Don't you Aunt Agnes me.

SHARON. Who are all these people?

AGNES. These people are all Lizzie's friends and neighbours come to see she gets a proper send-off.

SHARON. Joe! Do something!

JOE. Like what Sharon?

SHARON. It's always the same. If I want anything doing I have to do it myself. Right Charlie Wilson, outside for a moment. I want a word with you, in private. You too Joe McCullough!

They exit.

AGNES. Airs and graces! I knew her da when he hadn't an arse in his trousers.

Crossfade back to the vestibule. Out in the entrance hall, SHARON *shouts furiously at the* UNDERTAKER – *there is very little noise from the other room.*

SHARON. Right Charlie Wilson, explain yourself!

UNDERTAKER. I tried to stop it . . . I did, Mr McCullough . . . but your mother's sister . . . .

SHARON. Half-sister! We are the next of kin, not that interferin' oul biddy . . . .

JOE. I don't think Aunt Agnes meant no harm, Sharon . . . .

SHARON. She always means harm that one! She's evil . . . evil, so she is . . . .

JOE. Now calm down Sharon . . . .

SHARON. Calm down . . . calm down! After the evenin' I've had . . . music-boxes that won't stop playin' and you breakin' the only valuable ornament in that oul house of your mother's, and then comin' here, and you not man enough to stand up to that aunt of yours!

UNDERTAKER. Could I get you a cup of tea, Mrs McCullough . . . .

SHARON. No you could not! What you are goin' to do, is go in there and evict that mob.

UNDERTAKER. Me?

SHARON. You! (*There is a pause.*) My God you're as spineless as he is.

UNDERTAKER. It's not really my place to interfere with family.

SHARON. I won't let her get the better of me!

SERGEANT (*very quietly*). God bless all here. (SHARON *gasps, startled.*) I beg your pardon, madam. I didn't mean to startle you.

UNDERTAKER. Good evening, Sergeant Musgrave.

SERGEANT. Good evening, Mr Wilson. May I introduce Police Constable Patterson.

UNDERTAKER. Good evening, Constable Patterson.

CONSTABLE PATTERSON. Good evening, sir.

UNDERTAKER. Is there something wrong, Sergeant Musgrave?

SERGEANT. You tell me, Mr Wilson. We were just passin' and this keen-eared lad thought he heard a bit of a commotion. Is everything all right in here?

UNDERTAKER. I think so . . . I don't know . . . that is . . . .

SHARON. No everything is not all right, Sergeant. Tell him Joe!

JOE. Yes . . . well you see, Sergeant . . . tell him what, Sharon?

SHARON. Tell him there's a right crew in there, turning a respectable bereavement into . . . a party!

SERGEANT. Is that a fact now Mrs . . . ?

SHARON. McCullough, I'm the deceased's daughter-in-law.

SERGEANT. Well now, Mrs McCullough, if you'll just wait here in the vestibule, I will step inside and give Constable Patterson a chance to show me what he learned at the police training school.

Crossfade from the hall to the large room; the hum of conversation dies away.

Well now lad, what do you think? Is this a case for a quiet caution before we go on our way? Or do you think we should call for reinforcements and take the whole lot of them down to the station for questioning?

CONSTABLE. I . . . I don't know Sergeant . . . .

SERGEANT. You don't think this is an unlawful assembly then?

SARAH. Catch yourself on Jimmy Musgrave, you've known most of us here all your life.

SERGEANT. Hello there Sarah. How're you doin'?

SARAH. Can't complain Jimmy, can't complain . . . . What are you doin' out on the beat again?

SERGEANT. Just showin' this raw recruit around the area. Am I right in thinkin' the deceased's oul Lizzie McCullough?

SARAH. You are, God rest her.

SERGEANT. What's she doin' in here?

AGNES. You'd better ask that pair out there.

SERGEANT. Good evenin' Mrs Drumm, I didn't see you there, I'm sorry for your trouble.

AGNES. Much obliged, Jimmy. Would you like to view the remains?

SERGEANT. I'd be honoured, Mrs Drumm. You stand guard here Constable Patterson, make sure nobody gets out of hand. (*Receding.*)

Crossfade to the corpse – same atmosphere as before: quiet, reverential.

All the same, Lizzie's lookin' quare and well isn't she, Mrs Drumm?

AGNES. And why wouldn't she with all her friends gathered round her?

SERGEANT. Grand flowers them.

AGNES. Our Lizzie always loved a rose.

SERGEANT. Is there mustard on them ham sandwiches, Sarah?

SARAH. There is indeed, Jimmy.

JOHNNIE. Would you like a wee drink to wash that down, Jimmy?

SERGEANT. Not while I'm on duty, Johnnie . . . but I'll have a cup of tea if there's one goin'.

JOHNNIE (*going off*). Say no more Jimmy . . . no sooner said than done.

SERGEANT (*projected after him*). And I'm sure Constable Patterson could manage one if he was asked.

Crossfade back to the wake – chatter quite voluble again.

JOHNNIE. There ye are boys . . . two cups of the best tea on the road.

Sounds of the SERGEANT *drinking. He sighs contentedly. The rattle of cups and saucers.*

SERGEANT. Grand cup of tea that, Johnnie . . . (*The* CONSTABLE *splutters.*) It's a special brew they drink in these parts, son, you'll get used to it, given time.

JOHNNIE. Would you like a wee top up?

SERGEANT. Some other time, Johnnie. I think I'd better get the Constable back out on to the beat. He looks as if he could do with a bit of fresh air. Good night, Sarah. Good night, Mrs Drumm, and as I said I'm real sorry for your trouble.

SHARON *comes in, followed by* JOE, *and the* UNDERTAKER.

SHARON. And what about my trouble?

JOE. He said to wait in the hall, Sharon.

UNDERTAKER. Mrs McCullough.

SHARON. What are you goin' to do about this, Sergeant.

JOE. Sharon!

SERGEANT. You'd be Lizzie's son I take it?

JOE. That's right.

SERGEANT. Sorry for your trouble.

JOE. Thank you, Sergeant.

SHARON. I'm speakin' to you! What are you goin' to do about this?

SERGEANT. Are you makin' a complaint, Mr McCullough?

JOE. No.

SHARON. Joe!

SERGEANT. Are you makin' a complaint, Mr Wilson?

UNDERTAKER. Oh dear me no . . . indeed not, Sergeant . . . it's up to the family of the dear departed . . . I am only here to provide a service . . . whatever the family want . . . within reason . . . .

SERGEANT. Well then, as neither the next of kin, nor the proprietor are makin' a complaint, my hands is tied. I'm afraid, Constable Patterson, you're goin' to hafta qualify for your bravery medal on some other occasion. If I called back later, Sarah, would the teapot still be warm?

SARAH. Oh, I'd say you could depend on it, Jimmy.

SERGEANT. Right then, we'll be on our way. God bless all here.

SARAH. Goodnight, Jimmy.

The POLICEMEN *go.*

SHARON. Joe! Outside! I want to speak with you.

AGNES. Before yiz go, we'll need the key.

SHARON. What?

AGNES. The key . . . for our Lizzie's house. People'll be expectin' to come back after the funeral for the sit-down tea.

JOE. I haven't got the key.

AGNES. What do ye mean?

JOE. I'm sorry . . . Sharon . . . she likes things neat and tidy . . . I only did what I thought was for the best . . . .

SHARON. Joe McCullough! Don't you dare make apologies on my behalf to that . . . that . . . .

AGNES. I suppose you have the key, madam. Hand it over.

JOE. She hasn't got it . . . she . . . we . . . she got the lend of her brother's van this evenin' . . . that's what kept us . . . why we weren't here earlier . . . we cleared the house . . . we give the keys into the rentman on our way here . . . well, there was no point in payin' out another week's rent . . . .

AGNES (*quietly, contemptuously*). Get out of my sight.

SHARON. Don't you talk to my Joe like that.

AGNES. He's my nephew. I'll talk to him any way I want.

SHARON. You're a vindictive oul bitch. Ye always were.

JOE. Sharon . . . .

AGNES (*intones*). Sticks and stones may break my bones but your words cannot hurt me, for when I'm dead and in my grave you'll suffer for what you called me.

SHARON. Get away from me, you! Get away!

AGNES. You tried to get rid of my sister like an oul dog, so ye did. May she come back and haunt you for the rest of your days!

SHARON (*screams*). Joe!

She runs out. JOE runs after her calling her name. There is silence for a moment. Then AGNES laughs and gradually the other MOURNERS begin to laugh with her. JOHNNIE breaks and they begin the 'Doffer's Song' again. The singing builds in energy, culminating in cheering, clapping, laughter etc.

Crossfade to the funeral parlour. Late evening. The bulk of the MOURNERS have gone. Sounds of people saying goodnight, staggering outside.

DAVE. Hey Ma, me and Florence are just goin' to open up Madge's van for loadin' the stuff.

SARAH. Aye, well, don't the two of yiz be loiterin' long. I want you to organise the lifts for the coffin before your da and his cronies leave. You'll need six fit men in rotation.

DAVE. What lifts? Sure she's bein' cremated. My da can tuck the urn under his arm.

FLORENCE (*giggling*). Dave, you're awful . . . .

They go giggling.

SARAH (*shouts after him*). She'll be carried proper from here til the hearse and from the hearse till the crematorium . . . . I'm sorry about that Agnes.

AGNES. Pay no heed Sarah, he's young.

SARAH. He's drunk, but that's no excuse for irreverence.

AGNES. I'll just go and see how Lizzie's doin'.

SARAH. You do that, Agnes. I'll have a word with Mr Wilson about the vigil.

UNDERTAKER. I don't quite follow . . . the vigil?

SARAH. I'll be stayin' with Agnes the night. The rest of the weemin'll work out a rota for keepin' her and Lizzie company till Monday morning.

UNDERTAKER. Here all night. Staying?

SARAH. Aye, stayin'. You don't leave your dead alone, unprotected. They have to be watched over till the burial.

JOHNNIE. That was a grand evening, Mr Wilson. You done her proud. (*He shouts.*) Right lads, time to go home. Bring the dead men out to Madge's van, we'll take them back to the pub the morrow. That new barman's as mean as sin, Mr Wilson. Charged us on the bottles to make sure we brought back the empties.

Sounds of the crate being carried out and the MOURNERS *leaving.*

MADGE. Right Sarah. That's all the dishes washed up. Can I do anything else before I go?

SARAH. No thanks, Madge. You've been a tower of strength.

AGNES. You have that. God bless you, love.

MADGE. There's enough left in the kitchen to see yous through the night. I'll be here first thing in the mornin' to relieve you, Sarah.

SARAH. Thanks, Madge. Where's your Florence?

MADGE. She's sittin' in the van. Your Dave's keepin' her company. He offered to come home with us and unload the stuff.

UNDERTAKER. Excuse me . . . but will everybody be coming back tomorrow?

MADGE. Oh no, not on the sabbath, it wouldn't be proper. Just the women who'll be keepin' watch. (MADGE *goes.*)

UNDERTAKER. Is there anything else before I retire?

SARAH. No thank you, Mr Wilson. Everything's under control.

AGNES. We'll see you in the mornin', God willin'. Goodnight, son.

UNDERTAKER. Goodnight, ladies.

Fade out. Fade up on JOE *and* SHARON *in their car on the way to the funeral parlour.* SHARON *sneezes.*

JOE. You should of stayed in bed, Sharon.

SHARON. What, and given her the pleasure of sayin' I was too scared to turn up for the funeral? Oh no! We'll take our proper place as the first car behind the hearse.

JOE. We'll have to offer Aunt Agnes a seat in our car, Sharon.

SHARON. And offer her the chance of turnin' us down? You'll do no such thing, Joe McCullough. We'll keep ourselves to ourselves. I want nothin' to do with that rabble.

JOE. It's her proper place Sharon . . . .

SHARON. Her proper place is on a broomstick.

JOE. I should of been at the funeral parlour for the closin' of the coffin.

SHARON. I told you Joe. We are not gettin' out of this car until we get to the crematorium. And after that we are goin' straight home.

JOE. I feel . . . .

SHARON. What?

JOE. I feel . . . that I haven't said goodbye to my mother properly.

SHARON. What are you talkin' about? She's dead. Why does everybody keep goin' on as if she's still around and knows what we're all doin'!

Crossfade to the funeral parlour. The coffin is being screwed down.

AGNES. It's awful final, isn't it, once they screw the lid down.

UNDERTAKER. I'll just leave you two alone for a few minutes, then I'll send in the men to lift her.

He goes out. AGNES sighs.

AGNES. I suppose in time it'll be all crematoriums and funeral parlours. Strangers disposin' of your dead. At least you have childer, Sarah, to look after you when your time comes.

SARAH. I have only sons, Agnes. Men don't understand the importance of these things, and a daughter-in-law's no substitute for a daughter.

Crossfade to exterior acoustic: street noises, traffic, people talking.

JOHNNIE. Now, are ye sure the wreaths is right, Dave – family flowers on top of the coffin. Friend's and neighbour's on the roof rack.

DAVE. Yes, Da.

JOHNNIE. Right. Ye can close the hearse down now.

The door closes.

FLORENCE. Hello, Mr Maguire.

JOHNNIE. Mornin', Florence.

FLORENCE. I was just sayin' to my mammy, your Dave looks quare an' nice in a suit.

DAVE. You're not lookin' too bad yourself, Florence. You'd brighten any funeral.

JOHNNIE. In my day the weemin never went to the cemetery.

FLORENCE. How do you mean?

JOHNNIE. They stayed at home and got the sit-down tea ready for the men comin' back.

FLORENCE. Did they never see the grave then?

JOHNNIE. Oh yes, they went to the cemetery the followin' day and set out the wreaths nice and took a note of the cards to write the thank-you letters.

DAVE. There isn't goin' to be a graveside, Da.

JOHNNIE. Next thing you know, you'll be wantin' to take your turn with the men for liftin' the coffin.

DAVE. Well, they can take my turn anytime. My shoulder's wrecked.

JOHNNIE. Catch yourself on. A wee short lift like that. In the old days, we used to carry them for miles.

DAVE. From the funeral parlour to the hearse was far enough for me.

JOHNNIE. There's a knack for liftin' a coffin. You'll learn it as ye get older.

DAVE. I'm not plannin' to make a career of it, Da.

The hearse is revving up.

FLORENCE. We'd better get in the cars. Mr Wilson's revving up the hearse. I'll see you at Mrs Drumm's house later, Dave.

DAVE. I'll keep you a seat beside me at the sit-down tea.

JOHNNIE. No, ye'll not. The men eat first, and then the weemin.

DAVE. Why?

JOHNNIE. 'Cause that's the way it's done, that's why.

Crossfade to JOE *and* SHARON's *car. They are following behind the hearse.*

SHARON. Did you see the look that Agnes one give us, when we took our rightful place as the first car behind the hearse?

JOE. She looked awful old.

SHARON. She is old.

JOE. She looked pale, thin. I hope she's all right.

SHARON. She's with her cronies. They'll see her right.

JOE. They'll all be talkin' . . . sayin' she should of been in the family car . . . .

SHARON. Let them talk. When did she ever treat me like one of the family? Fifteen years we've been married, and she's never had a good word for me . . . .

JOE. I was only sayin' . . . .

SHARON. Well don't. And stop lookin' back at them. I'm not havin' your Aunt Agnes or that Sarah Maguire one, knowin' we're even takin' them under our notice. Them Maguires always had ideas above their station.

Cut to the Maguire car.

AGNES. See thon car of Joe's? Our Lizzie lent them the money for the deposit. They never paid it back.

SARAH. They'll never have any luck in it Agnes.

JOHNNIE. It's a bad do, Mrs Drumm, you not bein' in the front car.

AGNES. I prefer the car I'm in thanks Johnnie.

SARAH. You should of been asked.

AGNES. I'd of said no. I wouldn't demean myself.

SARAH. Dave!

DAVE. What?

SARAH. Will you concentrate on the drivin' and stop eyin' Florence in the mirror. You'll run intil the back of Joe's car!

AGNES. If it wasn't for the damage you'd do til yer own car, I'd say go right ahead, son.

DAVE (*laughing*). You're a terrible woman, Mrs Drumm.

Cut to JOE *and* SHARON's *car.*

SHARON. They're all laughin'.

JOE. What?

SHARON. Them Maguire's . . . don't look round! How many times do I have to tell you? Use the mirror if you want to see them. God, I'll be glad when this day's over.

The car stops.

What are ye doin'? What are ye stoppin' for?

JOE. The hearse has stopped, Sharon.

SHARON. We're nowhere near the crematorium. What's goin' on?

JOE. I dunno, Sharon. Charlie Wilson's gettin' out, so he is.

SHARON. Well you'd better get out too and find out what's happenin'.

Cut to the Maguire car during the following speech. The Maguire car stops.

AGNES. Are we there already Dave? I thought the crematorium was further out.

DAVE. The hearse has stopped.

JOHNNIE. An' Charlie Wilson's got out and so has Joe.

SARAH. Wind the window down, Johnnie.

The window is wound down.

JOHNNIE. They're lookin' under the bonnet of the hearse. An' yer woman Sharon's gettin' out and bearin' down on them like the wrath of God. You wanta see the face on her. It would melt snow.

SARAH. Away up Johnnie, an' see what's goin' on.

AGNES. We'll all go.

The car door opens.

SARAH. Do you think that's wise, Agnes?

AGNES. Lizzie's my sister. I've a right to know why she's come til a standstill.

Cut to the hearse.

SHARON. Joe, what are you doin'. You'll get oil on yer good suit.

JOE. Mr Wilson asked me to have a look at the engine . . .

SHARON. Fer what?

UNDERTAKER. I'm sorry, Mrs McCullough . . . I don't understand it. The hearse just stopped . . . an' it won't start again . . . and . . . .

SHARON. Petrol!

UNDERTAKER. Pardon?

SHARON. Did you check the petrol!

UNDERTAKER. The tank's full . . . I always fill her up the mornin' of a funeral . . . .

The footsteps of four people approaching.

JOHNNIE (*approaching*). Have you a problem, Mr Wilson?

UNDERTAKER. The engine died on me, and I can't see any reason why . . . .

SARAH (*approaching*). You have a look, Johnnie.

JOHNNIE. No problem.

SARAH. He's awful good with engines, Mr Wilson . . . .

SHARON. Is he a mechanic?

AGNES. Johnnie Maguire was repairin' oul beat up cars when you were still sellin' sticks after school.

SHARON. I wasn't talkin' to you . . . .

UNDERTAKER. It's not old. I only bought it last year. It's still under guarantee . . . .

AGNES. There's nuthin' wrong with yer vehicle, Mr Wilson. It's just our Lizzie showin' that pair they're not gettin' rid of her as easy as they thought . . . .

SHARON. Don't talk nonsense . . . .

AGNES. I warned ye she'd come back an' haunt ye Sharon . . . .

SHARON. Charlie Wilson! We haven't got all day. Joe's got to be back at his work this afternoon. This funeral has already cost him a mornin's wages . . . .

The music-box, very faint.

SHARON. Get away from me . . . .

JOE. What's the matter Sharon?

Silence for a moment.

SHARON. I thought . . . nuthin' . . . Charlie Wilson, away you over to that garage across the road an' get a proper qualified mechanic . . . and don't be puttin' the cost on our bill . . . if your hearse isn't roadworthy it's up to you to pay . . . .

The sounds of the music-box, very faintly, but longer this time. SHARON *screams.*

JOE. Sharon, what is it?

SHARON. It's her . . . it's her . . . Lizzie . . . across the road . . . look . . . look . . . gettin' onto that bus . . . look . . . .

The hearse engine roars into life.

JOHNNIE. I've got her goin', Mr Wilson!

AGNES (*quietly*). Atta girl Lizzie. You show her.

Sounds of SHARON *having hysterics. An excited hubbub of conversation.*

JOE. Sharon . . . Sharon . . . . Calm yourself . . . there's nobody there . . . .

SHARON. I want to go home . . . now . . . this minute . . . Joe!

JOHNNIE. What the divil's goin' on?

AGNES (*laughing*). Not the divil. Just our Lizzie.

SHARON. Don't you come near me, you witch . . . . Joe! Joe!

JOE. Sharon, you're makin' an eejit of yourself . . . get in the car . . . come on now . . . .

Sounds of SHARON *sobbing, getting into the car.* JOE *drives off.*

SARAH. See that Sharon one? She's just like her mother before her. That family always was awful high strung.

Fade out. Crossfade to SARAH's *house. A week later.*

DAVE. I'm away, Mammy. I'll see you later.

SARAH. Madge tells me that you and Florence are goin' to the pictures the night again, and I hear tell yous were at a disco last night.

DAVE. You couldn't fart on this road but everybody knows about it.

SARAH. I hope you don't use that sort of language in front of Florence, she's a nice, well brought-up wee girl. Are yous serious the two of ye?

DAVE. Mammy, it's only a week since I met her.

SARAH. Ah, there's many a good match was made at a wake. I noticed you weren't so anxious to leave once you clapped eyes on her.

DAVE. What are ye wantin' to marry me off for? Haven't ye got two daughters-in-law already?

SARAH. Aye, but I could take to Florence better than that other pair. She'd never be like Sharon . . . Lizzie soon put the fear of God into her though. Agnes buried Lizzie's ashes along with the weddin' ring and there wasn't a word about it.

DAVE. You don't think it really was Lizzie the day of the funeral . . . do you?

SARAH. Agnes warned them she'd come back and haunt them.

DAVE. Did you actually see her?

SARAH. I saw an old woman, and that's all any of them saw. But I'll tell you somethin' . . . as time passes, it'll become part of the folklore of this road, that on the day of her funeral, Lizzie McCullough appeared and made the hearse break down. The laugh of it is, that I don't think it would have occurred to anybody if Sharon hadn't put the idea into their heads in the first place.

DAVE. I'm away on. We're goin' for a drink before we go to the pictures. Did you get my blue jacket out of the cleaners? (*Receding.*)

SARAH. It's hangin' in the hall.

DAVE. Right, I've got it.

SARAH. By God you and your da'll miss me when I go . . . at least I think you will . . . sometimes I wonder though . . . .

DAVE *comes back into the room, putting on the jacket.*

DAVE. You know, you're gettin' awful vain in your old age, Ma.

SARAH. What?

DAVE. You're forever lookin' at yourself in the mirror these days.

SARAH. I'm not.

DAVE. You are. You're doin' it now.

SARAH. I was just fixin' my hair.

DAVE. I'll see you later. (*He goes off.*)

SARAH. Aye . . . have a good time . . . (*She calls his name as the door closes, pauses. She sighs.*) God, but you're gettin' old, Sarah Maguire . . . .

Fade up the music-box.

A MAN ALONE: ANTHONY

by Andrew Rissik

For my Mother

Andrew Rissik was born in 1955. He took a double first in English at Oxford in 1977, and was later elected a Senior Scholar at Christ Church, a position he resigned in 1979 when he came to London hoping to earn a living as a writer. He taught at a crammer in Knightsbridge, worked for Thames Television and the BBC, and has written critical pieces on radio, television, film and theatre for a wide range of magazines and newspapers, including *Time Out*, *The New Statesman*, *Harpers and Queen*, *The Times* and *The Independent*.
A television play, *Friends and Other Lovers*, was produced by Thames in 1980, and he has written five plays for BBC Radio, including the trilogy which makes up *A Man Alone*. Two further radio projects and a television play are currently under commission from the BBC.

A Man Alone: Anthony was first broadcast on BBC Radio 4 on
9 January 1986. The cast was as follows:

PHILIP TREMAYNE   Ronald Pickup
ANTHONY   Benedict Taylor
PHILIP'S FATHER   Patrick Troughton
LAURA   Tessa Peake-Jones
BOOKSELLER/PORTER   Brian Smith
MR TOMKIN   George Baker
PHILIP *as a boy*   Barnaby Rhys-Jones
ANTHONY *as a boy*   Thomas Amlot
CONSULTANT   Richard Durden

Director: Jeremy Mortimer
Running time, as broadcast: 56 minutes, 52 seconds

Author's Note

A Man Alone is a sequence of three plays and, although each was
designed to be self-contained, so that it might be heard singly, the
full narrative is only revealed by the trilogy as a whole. The story of
Anthony, which covers the years 1939 to 1956, continues through the
sixties and is brought up to date in the next two plays; and the
middle-aged Philip, who is here merely a narrating voice, is the
embattled central character of the third. What you read, therefore, is
only Act One of a three-Act drama, but the story which is told in this
play underpins and overshadows almost everything that happens in
the other two. I don't know that it's the best of the three, but it sets
out the ground for what follows and, read purely by itself, it
probably makes the most sense.

The noise of a bottle being opened, a slug of whisky poured into a glass. The glass is picked up, PHILIP *drinks. He puts the glass down. A moment.* PHILIP *is 54, a little drunk, alone, not particularly happy. We don't know where we are or what time of day it is. We are in a small, book-lined study. It's late.*

PHILIP (*voice over*). I get home usually at around half past five. I don't like to be too precise about my hours. I like a good, lazy wander in the afternoon. These days I work in the mornings, have a light lunch, then go and nose around a few bookstores. Sometimes I find something I've written.

At once we're in a little shop. PHILIP *picks up a book, takes it to the counter.*

PHILIP. How much is this?

SHOPKEEPER. Let me see, sir. That's 20p, sir.

PHILIP (*low*). That's an absolute bloody disgrace. Right. I'll take it.

SHOPKEEPER. Very good, sir.

At once we are back, in the dark, with PHILIP *talking to us.*

PHILIP (*voice over*). When I get back I make myself a light supper. I'm not a good cook. I manage an omelette or some scrambled eggs. Then I have a drink or two. I can't get to sleep. Sometimes I doze off in my chair but in bed, where I'm supposed to sleep, I hardly sleep at all. I have some pills. They don't work. Last week I went to see a specialist.

Into this scene at once. A Harley Street consulting-room; a kind but rather distant consultant. The obvious sounds.

CONSULTANT. There's nothing physically wrong with you. Or nothing unusual in a man of 54. You're a stone overweight. And you drink too much. But I'm sure you can put that right yourself. How do you feel?

PHILIP. I feel terrible.

CONSULTANT. I think you're somewhat tired. You've been
   bereaved recently, I understand.

PHILIP. Yes.

CONSULTANT. It may not be very comforting to hear this, but
   I think in the circumstances you're doing rather well. You've had
   the stuffing knocked out of you. You say you don't sleep?

PHILIP. Not very well, no.

CONSULTANT. That's no cause for alarm. If the body needed the
   rest you'd sleep all right then. I think this is a mild case of
   emotional exhaustion. I'll give you some pills.

PHILIP. Right.

CONSULTANT. Mr Tremayne. I say this to a lot of my patients.
   Life is a vale of tears, I'm afraid. There's not much a doctor can
   do about that. Now. Don't take these with alcohol. And I'd like
   to see you again in about a month.

We lose this immediately. We are back with PHILIP *talking to us, out of
the darkness.*

PHILIP (*talk over*). I make an appointment, of course. One does as
   one's told. Shall I keep it? I doubt it. What do doctors know
   about anything, for God's sake. They only want your money. In
   my hands I cradle the first edition I bought today for 20p. I wrote
   that in 1964. I look at it. It seems an awfully long time ago. Still.
   I read for a bit. Then I go up to bed. I read for a bit there. I turn
   out the light. Do I sleep? Of course I bloody well don't. At twenty
   past five I have half a bottle of scotch. That does the trick all
   right. At twelve I wake feeling as if I've been punched in the head.
   Going downstairs I catch sight of myself in the mirror. Not a
   pretty picture at all. If I go on like this I've had it. Sometimes,
   during the day, I think of dropping what I'm doing, simply
   stopping whatever it is, and screaming. But I don't. I don't scream
   because inside me, somewhere, there's a small, private, protected
   scream that's never released. Cheers. Your very good health.

He pours himself another drink. A sense of us closing in on him now.

God knows what's gone wrong. I can't explain it. I've not been all
that good with other people, I do see that now. (*A moment.*) When
I was 8 I had a headmaster called Mr Tomkin. Sometimes you'd
go to his study to get the cane. This wasn't unusual. Everyone got
the cane sometime or other. But Tomkin tried to be as pleasant
about it as possible. I remember what a friend of mine used to say.

*Immediately we are with the two small boys, waiting nervously outside the
study. The clatter of the school in the distance.*

ANTHONY. It's easy for him to talk. It's not his bum, is it?

PHILIP. How many do you think we'll get?

ANTHONY. I should think three each is a pretty good guess. If he gives me six I'll sock him in the mouth.

PHILIP (*wide-eyed*). You wouldn't dare.

ANTHONY. Don't bank on it. Look. Are you going to knock or shall I?

PHILIP. You knock.

ANTHONY. Here goes.

He knocks, loud and clear. The study door snaps open almost instantaneously. TOMKIN *looms.*

TOMKIN. Ah, the heavenly twins. Moore and Tremayne. I bet your knees are turning to jelly. Now look. If you talk very loudly after lights out you can't expect to get away with it every time. That's not cricket, is it?

ANTHONY. No, sir.

TOMKIN. So no hard feelings. But remember, the two of you. Learn from your mistakes. Always learn from your mistakes. You're neither of you stupid. You know that, don't you?

PHILIP.　　｝Yes, sir.
ANTHONY.　

TOMKIN. Right. No point in hanging about. You first, Moore, if you'd be so kind.

And we lose this as PHILIP *narrates. The scene changes.*

PHILIP (*voice over*). Anthony Moore was my best friend. We did virtually everything together, and were often in trouble. I didn't call him Anthony. I called him Moore. He called me Tremayne. We never used Christian names, except sometimes in the holidays. He'd been at the school a term longer than me.

At once a new scene. TOMKIN *is calling the register at morning assembly. A large hall with an echo.* TOMKIN *goes fast.*

TOMKIN. Stanton.

BOY. Sir.

TOMKIN. Stevenage, J.

BOY. Sir.

TOMKIN. Matron's got something for that disgusting athlete's foot of yours, so go and see her after this assembly, will you?

BOY. Yes, sir.

TOMKIN. Stevenage, R.

BOY. Sir.

TOMKIN. Tremayne. (*A moment.*)

PHILIP. Here, sir. Sorry, sir.

TOMKIN. Wake up, Tremayne. When I was at school my headmaster had a great big cane and we wouldn't have dared go to sleep.

ANTHONY (*speaking out*). We don't dare either, sir. For exactly the same reason.

A moment or two. ANTHONY *does things like this.* TOMKIN *is amused.*

TOMKIN. I don't think anyone asked you to speak, Moore.

ANTHONY. Oh, I don't wait to be asked, sir.

TOMKIN. I'll whack you for something before the term's out, just you wait and see.

ANTHONY. You already have, sir.

TOMKIN. Have I really? I'd forgotten. What had you done?

ANTHONY. Talking after lights out, sir.

TOMKIN. That's a terrible crime, isn't it? Why do you do it, you foolish boy?

ANTHONY. I get bored, sir.

TOMKIN. I was never bored at your age. I was much too busy to be bored. I was out and about, playing cricket and rugger, doing everything under the sun, all the time.

ANTHONY. I'm sure you were, sir.

TOMKIN. Are you being rude?

ANTHONY. No, sir. I was agreeing with you, sir.

TOMKIN. Well, kindly shut up while I finish the register.

And on he goes. We lose this as PHILIP *narrates over.*

PHILIP (*voice over*). No one ever disliked Anthony. Even Tomkin seemed rather fond of him. But there were times when we all found him irksome and maladroit. He was tall for his age and he walked in a shambling, dislocated way that was soon parodied throughout the school. And his hair was dark and unmannerly and, whatever the barber did, it was still a shock of black, a sort of plumage that marked him out. On the rugger field, in those raw winter evenings, he was a hopeless case and he infuriated Tomkin.

At once an exterior acoustic. A rugger pitch in the gathering winter twilight. TOMKIN *is on the touchline, perched on a shooting stick, bawling instructions.*

TOMKIN. That's right! That's better! That's more like it! Oh, well played, Tremayne. Well done, boy. Now come on. Follow it. FOLLOW IT! That's the way. Oh, come on, Moore. Come on, you idle boy! Run run run run run. Faster, Moore. You've got great strong legs, boy. Come on. You've got more wind than that. Feet feet feet feet feet!

The REFEREE *blows his shrill little whistle.*

Oh, Moore. You're a disgrace to your side. We shall have to do something about you, Moore. Off you go. Showers every one of you. I want no wet hair at tea. Tremayne!

PHILIP. Sir.

TOMKIN. Over here, boy.

PHILIP *goes over, stands by* TOMKIN.

I'm very pleased with you, Tremayne. You're an absolutely excellent player.

PHILIP. Thank you, sir.

TOMKIN. But allow me to give you some advice. Go down for those shots. Right down. D'you see?

PHILIP. Yes, sir.

TOMKIN. Like this. Right down. Do you see? A much better way of doing it.

PHILIP. Yes, sir.

TOMKIN. You can tell your friend Moore that he can parade in my study after tea. I'm not having idleness on the field.

PHILIP. He does try, sir. He tries awfully hard.

TOMKIN. Does he?

PHILIP. Oh yes, sir.

TOMKIN. Well, why doesn't he succeed then? You do.

PHILIP. He's no good at it, sir.

TOMKIN. Ah, but does he want to be? That's the point.

PHILIP. Yes, sir.

TOMKIN. Now you cut along. You're a generous lad. Tell him he's only escaped death by a whisker this time.

PHILIP. Right-oh, sir.

And we lose this as PHILIP *narrates. Underneath, we bleed through to the next scene.*

PHILIP (*voice over*). I find it difficult now to account for how precisely we became friends. I think it had something to do with the location of my form room, which was on the ground floor next to the dining-hall. I was often the first changed and I'd go in and sit by the fire and wait for the bell for tea. One afternoon Anthony came in and flung himself in the master's chair and sat staring at me with those green, unquiet eyes of his. He loathed rugger. He asked me what on earth I saw in the game.

We're in a small, rather bare form room. A fire blazes in the grate.
The to and fro of boys in the passage outside.

ANTHONY. Charging up and down all afternoon chasing that disgusting piece of old leather. It's insane. Two thousand years of civilisation and we're still doing things like that. Do you know how it all started? Rugby and football I mean?

PHILIP. No. How?

ANTHONY. Well, when criminals had their heads cut off, the mob used to put the head in a leather bag and kick it around for a lark.

PHILIP. Really?

ANTHONY. Oh, yes. That's probably why Tomkin admires it so much. It's his prehistoric instincts coming out. Anyway. I'm hopeless at it. He'll just have to keep whacking me. I've no co-ordination at all. Though I'm not bad with a twelve-bore.

PHILIP. Do your people allow you to use one?

ANTHONY. My father's dead. Mama doesn't care what I do. We sit up each night in the hols and play bridge, but that's illegal here. I suppose Old Bottom Thrasher thinks we're going to get terribly depraved.

PHILIP. Is that what you call him?

ANTHONY. It's his initials. He's called Oliver Bennet Tomkin. So I think it goes rather well. He's an idiot, of course. He should be grazing in a field not running a school.

PHILIP (*smile*). He's all right. I quite like him.

ANTHONY. Schoolmasters are vermin, on the whole. They should send people with ferrets to get rid of them. You know, Tomkin caught me reading *Murder in the Cathedral* last term and do you know what he said? He said, 'Ah, Moore, you'd better put that sixpenny thriller away before I give you a taste of the stick.'

PHILIP. Isn't *Murder in the Cathedral* a sort of play? Or something?

ANTHONY. There. Even you know and you're in Form 1. But Tomkin never reads anything but the racing pages of the *Daily Telegraph* and so he's never heard of it. I shall come back here when I'm a great strapping man of twenty and tan his arse for him.

PHILIP. You wouldn't dare.

ANTHONY. Oh, yes, I would. (*Shouting.*) Come here, Tomkin! I'm going to tan your arse, Tomkin!

PHILIP. For Pete's sake, Moore, he'll hear us.

ANTHONY. No, he won't. He's watching the rugger. Come here,

Tomkin! I'll tan your arse for you, Tomkin!

The door snaps open. TOMKIN *stands. A horrible pause. His manner is suave and deadly.*

TOMKIN. Ah, Moore. Allow me to return the compliment. Into the study, if you'd be so kind.

ANTHONY (*ashen*). Yes, sir.

TOMKIN. Never make threats you're in no position to carry out. (*To* PHILIP:) Were you making a racket too, Tremayne.

PHILIP. No, sir.

TOMKIN. I thought not.

He goes out with ANTHONY. *We cut at once to the dining-hall at tea-time.* BOYS *collecting their milk.* ANTHONY *is chastened, tearful but, beneath it, venomously angry.*

PHILIP. How many did you get?

ANTHONY. Three. He thinks its funny. My mother sent me here because she thought I'd get an education but in fact it's like being at a brothel for flagellants.

We lose this.

PHILIP (*voice over*). In the holidays Anthony came to stay with me. My mother had left us when I was only a year old and my father, who simply behaved as if she had never existed, thought it healthy that I should have some company of my own age. During that quiet, pleasant summer of 1939 we used to sit on the veranda as tea was served and my father would chuckle to himself as Anthony talked.

In on this at once. Wasps buzz idly about the jam. PHILIP'S FATHER *is a mild-mannered, rather formal man in whom a great sense of fun lies very near the surface.*

FATHER. I think you do your headmaster an injustice, Anthony.

ANTHONY. I don't think I do, sir.

PHILIP (*cross*). Will somebody please tell me what a brothel for flagellants is.

FATHER. I think, old chap, that that's a secret that Anthony and I shall keep to ourselves. Master Moore is quite inappropriately well-versed in the ways of the world.

ANTHONY. All you have to do is read books.

FATHER. That depends on the sort of books you read.

ANTHONY. At home we have a book room. You can go in and read anything you like. My father used to collect them before he died.

PHILIP. He could hardly have collected them afterwards, could he?

ANTHONY (*smile*). Shut up, you prize oaf.

FATHER. I must say I'd very much l'ke to have collected books.
But I've never found the time or the money. There's so much else
to do these days.

ANTHONY. My father was a man of leisure but I don't really
remember him all that well.

FATHER. A man of leisure?

ANTHONY. That's what Mama says. I think that's where the money
came from.

FATHER. But what did he do?

ANTHONY. I don't think he did anything. I think that was why
he was so rich.

PHILIP's FATHER *laughs. A brief silence.*

FATHER. Well then. What are you two chaps proposing to do
tomorrow?

PHILIP. I thought we'd go sculling on the river.

FATHER. Can Anthony row?

ANTHONY. I'm learning, sir.

PHILIP. I'm teaching him to feather his oar.

FATHER. Goodness me.

PHILIP. He says it's more difficult that it looks.

FATHER. I should say so.

ANTHONY. I have problems with my co-ordination, sir. Everything
looks so easy until I try it.

FATHER. Well. If there's a war you'll have to learn things like that.
They'll march you up and down until you do.

ANTHONY. Do you think there will be a war, sir?

FATHER. I rather think there may. The Russians have dropped us in
the soup. We made them a perfectly reasonable offer and they've
shown us the door.

PHILIP. They need the Tsar back.

ANTHONY (*suddenly serious*). Do you know what sort of man
the Tsar was?

FATHER. Oh, the Tsar was a perfectly well-meaning sort of man,
Anthony. But he didn't understand his people. He never knew
what they felt or thought or wanted. You've read some history.
He wasn't unlike Louis XVI. Anyway. Stalin has signed with the
Germans. And that means that Herr Hitler may do as he pleases.
It's not a pleasant prospect.

ANTHONY. What'll you do if there's a war, sir?

FATHER. I expect they'll find something for me to do. I can't join up, though. I'm past the age and I'd never get a clean bill of health.

PHILIP. Papa fought the Pathans in India.

ANTHONY. Did you really, sir? Were they ferocious?

FATHER. They were certainly very hardy. And of course they knew the country better than we did. And when we first went out none of us were used to the heat.

PHILIP. Papa was a magistrate when he was only twenty-one.

FATHER (*smile*). That's right. Awfully big and important. I got pneumonia in the end, and then bronchitis and so they had to pack me off home.

ANTHONY. Did you want to stay?

FATHER. I'd like to have stayed, yes. There was so much to get to know. And if you were a British officer it was really rather pleasant.

ANTHONY. Natives in turbans cleaning your boots.

FATHER (*smile*). There was more to it than that.

PHILIP. There's a stuffed tiger in the attic. Papa shot that.

FATHER. Well, actually, several of us shot it. But I was allowed to keep it. I was the senior officer.

ANTHONY. I've never been anywhere. I've hardly seen anything. I have been to Paris but everyone's done that, haven't they?

FATHER. I haven't. Can you speak French?

ANTHONY. Oui, monsieur. Je le parle à merveille.

FATHER. That's not bad. You're quite a sophisticated young man. Well. France is where Hitler will want to go pretty soon. Whether he can cross the Channel is another matter. Let's hope it's all academic, anyway.

We lose this. PHILIP *narrates.*

PHILIP (*voice over*). Each morning we used to go down to the river and pretend to be pirates. Anthony painted a skull and crossbones on an old curtain and he used to stand in the bows and yell at anyone who went past.

Into this immediately. A small rowing-boat which PHILIP *is rowing.* ANTHONY *yells. He's loving every minute of this.*

ANTHONY. Get up aloft, you dogs! Cram on the canvas! Every stitch! Run up the Black Flag! Any man who contradicts me, I'll spit him through his gizzard with a marlinspike! I'll have no mutiny aboard my ship! Get aloft!

We lose this as PHILIP *narrates. Under it they beach the boat and walk back toward the house.*

PHILIP (*voice over*). At around mid-morning we'd head back toward the house for something to eat. That day, as we turned the corner of the drive, my father was standing in the porch calling to us.

Into this at once. PHILIP *is chatting away to* ANTHONY. *They plod along.*

PHILIP. You've got to pull on both oars at the same time. Otherwise you just go round and round.

FATHER (*distant*). Philip! Anthony! You two boys!

ANTHONY. That's your old man.

PHILIP. What's up, do you think?

ANTHONY. Hitler I reckon.

They race up to the house. PHILIP's FATHER *is grave. He bustles them into the drawing-room.*

FATHER. Into the drawing-room. As fast as your legs will carry you.

PHILIP. What's up, Papa?

FATHER. You'll soon see.

ANTHONY. It's the Germans, isn't it, sir?

PHILIP's FATHER *doesn't answer this. We are now in the drawing-room. The wireless is on and Neville Chamberlain's famous broadcast has already begun. We catch the phrase about a state of war.*

PHILIP. Gosh.

FATHER. That's that then. I expect you two think it's jolly exciting but I'm afraid I don't.

He turns the wireless off. A moment or two. As usual ANTHONY *breaks the silence.*

ANTHONY. Do you think Mr Chamberlain was any use to us, sir?

FATHER. Oh, I'm sure he did his level best. But he's a provincial politician, not a diplomat. He was never going to put the wind up Herr Hitler. I doubt he'll be Prime Minister for long.

ANTHONY. Who do you think we'll have?

FATHER. I expect we'll have Halifax. He seems the obvious choice.

ANTHONY. What about Churchill?

FATHER. Churchill's too damn difficult. He's not liked enough. War's an awful business. We seem to have learnt nothing. And this time we'll all be involved, all of us, everyone, everywhere, everything. You're lucky to be at school. You're lucky to be young.

PHILIP. I wish I could fight.

ANTHONY. So do I, sir. I'm quite useful with a shotgun.

FATHER (*a hint of a smile*). Well. It may go on for a very long time.

*And we lose this. A bell sounds. We are in the assembly hall at school.
A general murmur. Everyone is waiting for* TOMKIN *to speak.*
ANTHONY *whispers to* PHILIP.

ANTHONY. He's going to harangue us. He's going to tell us our duty.

PHILIP. What's wrong with that?

ANTHONY. You'll see.

There is silence now, the school waits. TOMKIN *clears his throat.
A moment.*

TOMKIN. Gentlemen. Some of us have fought the Hun before.
Some of us know how careful and methodical they are. Some of
us already know the firmness of their purpose. This is not a
matter of Britain going to war to defend her own interests. No, by
no means. What we are fighting for here is the freedom and
liberty of the whole of Europe. We are laying down our lives so
that others may live. We are doing this because we believe that
everyone has a right to rule themselves on their own, in their own
way. We do not see why the world should submit to the yoke of
Nazi tyranny. We are not fighting simply to defend ourselves,
I tell you. Incredible as it may seem to some of you now, who
know the size and industry of the German machine, we are
fighting not for today or tomorrow but for an ultimate and
complete victory. And I say also that although our part in this
may be small and menial we shall pursue it with the same
unflagging energy and zeal that will surely distinguish every one
of our young men on the field or at sea or in the air.

At this point, quite spontaneously, the school claps its headmaster.

We will now sing hymn number 84 in the school hymn-book.

*The school piano strikes up 'I vow to thee my country'. Everyone sings with
patriotic fervour.* ANTHONY *whispers to* PHILIP, *quiet but urgent.*

ANTHONY (*whispering to* PHILIP). If that's true, what are we doing
in Africa? What are we doing in India? Does anyone ever think
about these things?

PHILIP. Shut up.

ANTHONY. I know we're right to be at war, I know we're right to
try and stop Hitler, but why should we have to listen to that
stupid old man making speeches? He's not going to have to fight.
He can say what he likes. He won't have to prove it.

And we lose this. PHILIP, *his* FATHER *and* ANTHONY *sit round the
dining-room table.* PHILIP's FATHER *talks with quiet gravity.*

FATHER. Oh, come now, Anthony. You are surely not suggesting that our presence in India, in Africa, in Canada, in Australia is remotely comparable to what Hitler is up to in Europe. Hitler is trying to subjugate the world. And I believe, I do believe, that we are trying to educate it. Your political interest is commendable. And I admire your spirit. But you really know far too little of the world. And it's certainly not the fault of the British cause that your headmaster is a man of limited intelligence who is merely attempting to make the best of a very alarming situation.

ANTHONY (*quiet*). He's a fool.

FATHER. No, he's not. He's an everyday sort of man trying to do his best.

PHILIP's FATHER's *mildness of manner does give* ANTHONY *some pause for thought. A moment or two.*

PHILIP. Tomkin says they're going to start bombing us. Flying over and dropping bombs.

FATHER. I'm afraid that's only too likely.

PHILIP. He says they want to hit the aerodromes. He says what they do is, they drop their incendiaries first, so they can see what they're doing, and then they just fill the sky with high explosives.

FATHER. I imagine that's a pretty fair assessment.

ANTHONY. Supposing we get killed.

FATHER. Supposing you don't. Look at it that way.

We lose this at once. We fade through to the muffled thunder of a nearby air-raid. This continues under the following.

PHILIP (*voice over*). The school was near the river and we dreaded moonlit nights because the moon shone on the surface of the Thames and the bombers could see their way by the light of it. Tomkin took to handing out little paper bags of toffee, which you were supposed to chew if a bomb dropped, to absorb the impact he told us. But at the first wail of the air-raid sirens we all crammed our mouths with toffees, we all chewed and sucked and spat them at each other, and soon Tomkin was issuing us with little squares of rubber. We could chew those. They tasted much less pleasant.

We're in a crowded school dormitory. The air-raid continues in the distance.

PHILIP. Are you still awake?

ANTHONY. Can anyone sleep with this din going on?

PHILIP. It's quarter past twelve. Porter's asleep and Stevenage is actually snoring.

ANTHONY. There's been a direct hit on something near the river. I've just seen this whole mountain of flame.

PHILIP. Where?

ANTHONY. There. People are probably dying.

PHILIP. I say. Hard cheese.

ANTHONY. We could easily be next. You know, by mistake. Someone dumping their bombs. It wouldn't be hard cheese then.

PHILIP. I don't believe anyone you know gets killed. I just don't. I'm sure I'm going to be all right. (*A moment.*) What are you reading?

ANTHONY. *Lord Jim.*

PHILIP. The one about the coward?

ANTHONY. That's right. Except that he's not a coward. He's morally very strong. Or at least I think so.

There's a sudden very loud bang, closer than before.

ANTHONY. I told you. Some *swinehund* dumping his bombs. I'm getting a little tired of reading. I think I'd like to write something myself.

PHILIP. Can you do that?

ANTHONY. It's not as easy as I thought. I've been writing down bits and pieces, descriptions of things I've seen. I've got an awfully good bit about Tomkin. But often they don't turn out very well. I don't think I'll ever write a novel. I'll write about people. Things that happen to you. Characters you meet.

PHILIP. You could write for a newspaper.

ANTHONY. Well, yes, but people throw newspapers away. I'd like to be remembered.

PHILIP. Have you got the thing about Tomkin?

ANTHONY. It's in my locker.

PHILIP. Can I read it?

ANTHONY. I might let you. But I don't want him finding it and taking it away. We can sneak off to the cricket pavilion tomorrow afternoon if you're game.

PHILIP. I'm game.

Interior acoustic. The cluttered cricket pavilion. A hollow, old sound.
PHILIP *and* ANTHONY *clear things to sit.*

ANTHONY. Right. No one'll find us here. And it's an hour to the tea bell. But watch the window just in case. Sing out *cave* if you see anyone. (*He opens his exercise book.*) By the way, say if you think it's bad. I welcome honest criticism.

PHILIP. Get on with it.

ANTHONY (*reading*). 'Normally, in his day-to-day business about the school, Mr Tomkin walks with an easy swagger, like an admiral patrolling his quarterdeck, and he swishes the air with his right hand, as if reaching for an invisible, phantom cane. I admit that when he smiles he has the bluff charm of a good professional Santa Claus, but he becomes angry too quickly, like an infuriated infant, and his rages are the rages of the mad Roman emperors of old. When squared up to by a rich or important parent, or an influential governor, his manners are impeccable and if it is possible to grovel discreetly this is what Mr Tomkin does. (*He stops.*) Well, that's it. Is it awful?

PHILIP. It's exactly like him. Anyone would know. It sounds . . . .

ANTHONY. Yes?

PHILIP. Well, it sounds as if it was written by a grown-up. I mean, I wouldn't know you'd written it at all. It's awfully good.

ANTHONY. It's a parody of real writing, really, but I'll probably grow out of that. Mama says I can't expect to write anything all that good at twelve. People just don't. But the thing is . . . the thing is I can't invent anything. I don't seem to be able to make things up. I'd love to write a Dickens or a Conrad but I just can't get started.

PHILIP. I couldn't do it at all.

ANTHONY. You get very good marks for your compositions.

PHILIP. That's subjects. If the subject is exciting, it's easy. And I don't know half so many words. And I never get the grammar quite right.

ANTHONY. I think you may turn out to be better than me.

PHILIP. I could never have written that.

ANTHONY. Oh, I just pick things up quickly. That's all it is. It's a knack.

A moment as he broods. He moves to the window.

I don't know whether I shall get married. I'm not sure I'm the marrying sort. It might be fun to have a mistress. Or just a very close friend. I think I probably need people. I need them round me. But the problem is . . . I don't actually like them very much. Do you?

We lose this after a moment. We are in the crowded assembly hall at the end of ANTHONY's *last term.*

PHILIP (*voice over*). To no one's great surprise, Anthony won the top scholarship to Harrow. I was set to take the same exam a term or two later, and so I hoped to be there with him. At prizegiving that term Tomkin gave him a splendid send off.

TOMKIN *is giving his leavers' speech. It's the end of term and there are general high spirits.*

TOMKIN. And last there is the skeletal but somewhat frightening figure of Moore. Now, Moore may be no athlete, I think we all know that . . .

A little good-natured laughter.

. . . but Moore can do a great many things the rest of you can't. Moore is not only clever, which is something we know from the Harrow scholarship, but he is also sophisticated, well-read and, to all of us here, very learned indeed. And, since this is his last day in the school, I think I can tell him that he is probably the cleverest boy I have ever taught. We all know him to be modest and generous, and we here, his teachers and his friends, expect great things of him in the world outside. It now remains for me to give him the leavers' book, a complete Shakespeare, which I know he will enjoy. Thank you.

There is clapping. We lose this as PHILIP *narrates.*

PHILIP (*voice over*). That night I sat reading in the library. At length Anthony came in and, with a preoccupied sort of expression, sat down next to me and looked me in the eye.

Into this at once. The quiet library. The hubbub of the school in the distance.

ANTHONY. Do you have any idea of how I feel about you?

PHILIP. What . . . what do you mean?

ANTHONY. Oh, I don't know. I have a friend, I suppose. I seem to be of some value to you. I'm awfully grateful. I couldn't be more grateful. It's probably such a little thing to you . . . but it isn't to me.

And then we lose the scene. PHILIP *narrates.*

PHILIP (*voice over*). And then, without putting his hand upon my shoulder as I feared he might, without any demonstration whatsoever of outward emotion, he got up and left the room. After he had gone I sat for a time without moving. I thought about what he had said and meant and what had passed. I began to ask myself if this was love, this feeling that I had awoken in him, this strange closeness that I felt, what was this, so unfamiliar to me, this curious and rather crooked emotion, this sense of a bond where once no bond had existed, what was it? Later, I tried to return to my book but my mind was not on it, and I drifted into other, more pressing patterns and thoughts. Hours later, in our large, cold dormitory, I undressed and climbed between the sheets but I was still in some faint trance, some absorption that I could not explain rationally. I lay there in the dark for a long time that night and, even then, I could make nothing of this new emotion, I could not tell from where it came or the manner of its operation, but I knew that I was, in some respect, an entirely changed person, someone who had perceived in the order of things a new and compelling perspective, a young man who had lost in a few hours the absolute separateness of childhood. And then I fell asleep and woke the next morning with a new vigour and energy and understanding.

And then, in the silence, VERA LYNN *singing 'When the lights go on again'. A few bars of this and then a rushing montage of sound. A steam train hurtling past us. It arrives, hissing and clanking, at Oxford Station. Spires, clocks and bells.* PHILIP *is arriving there in late 1952. He is driven from the station. He stands at the Porter's Lodge.*

PORTER. Yes, sir?

PHILIP. Tremayne. Philip Tremayne.

PORTER. Yes indeed. Peckwater Quad. Staircase two, room one. I'll take you over.

PHILIP. Thank you.

PORTER. There's drinks for freshmen in hall at a quarter to seven, sir.

PHILIP. Oh. Right.

A sense of them crossing the quad. PHILIP *makes conversation.*

Well. This is certainly a change after National Service.

PORTER. I can believe it only too well, sir. Which service were you in?

PHILIP. The RAF. At a base in Uxbridge.

PORTER. That was my service, too, sir, during the war. I can't say I enjoyed it. Those bloody Flight Sergeants. Yes, Flight, no, Flight, Flight bloody this and Flight bloody that. 'Course I was a sergeant myself by the end.

They walk on for a moment.

PHILIP. I've got a rather old friend up here too so I hope it's going to be fun.

PORTER. What would his name be, sir?

PHILIP. Anthony Moore.

PORTER. Oh yes.

PHILIP. Do you know him?

PORTER. I like to think I know every gentleman in the college, sir. Mr Moore's quite a personality.

Then suddenly ANTHONY *speaks. He's spotted* PHILIP *and the* PORTER *crossing the quad.*

ANTHONY. Good evening, Reg. I'm afraid it's speak of the devil.

PORTER. Good evening, sir. I understand you know Mr Tremayne.

ANTHONY. Certainly I do. (*To* PHILIP:) I saw the two of you struggling across the quad. I have to be somewhere else in about twenty minutes. But I did just want to say hello. I heard from the lodge you'd be here on the six o'clock train.

PHILIP (*smile*). It's very good to see you again, Anthony, it really is.

PORTER. I imagine you two gentlemen will have plenty to talk about. Goodnight, sir. Goodnight, Mr Tremayne.

He goes.

PHILIP. Goodnight. And thank you.

ANTHONY. Night, Reg. (*To* PHILIP:) He can be a rather bloody-minded sort. I don't think any of them here have forgiven me for putting a swan in the fountain last term. They just found it there, swimming around, with a black bow tie round its neck. Took them all morning to get it out.

PHILIP. You've changed a bit.

ANTHONY. I'm in my element, which I never really was at Harrow.

PHILIP. Byron was an Old Harrovian.

ANTHONY. Byron was also a bloody aristocrat. How was the cricket?

PHILIP (*smile*). The cricket was glorious.

ANTHONY. You should have stayed there. You should never have left. You should have played for the Eleven and been Head of the School for the rest of your life.

PHILIP. Perhaps. I was rather good at it.

ANTHONY. Listen. You must come to some meetings. You must come and hear me speak. I do quite a lot of it. I'm a bit of a celebrity. There are people you must meet.

PHILIP. People?

ANTHONY. Women. There's a woman here called Laura Kennedy who must be the single most brilliant person of her year and who happens, also, to be quite extraordinarily beautiful.

PHILIP. Really?

ANTHONY. Oh, I'm very smitten. I really am. She talks almost as well as I do.

PHILIP. She'll never be short of enemies, then, will she?

They smile. ANTHONY *claps his hands on* PHILIP's *shoulders. They stand for a moment, surveying each other.*

ANTHONY. Philip. My dear friend. It really is wonderful to see you again.

PHILIP (*voice over*). My first weeks in Oxford were heady and chaotic. Anthony took me everywhere. Often I went to places simply to hear him speak.

The debating chamber of the Oxford Union.

ANTHONY *is speaking. He is relaxed, louche and frivolous.*

ANTHONY. Art. Sponsorship of the arts. It's clearly Mr Churchill's obligation to pursue this with the same vigour and enthusiasm with which he pursues everything else. His government must support the artist without discrimination. More depends upon it than is sometimes imagined. If the government of Germany had allowed Hitler into art school, had encouraged him, had asked him to design buildings, had commissioned paintings from him, then Europe might be a happier place today. Hitler, after all, for all his faults, was a better painter than Churchill.

There is general laughter, though not overdone. We fade through to a little later. An anteroom of some sort. Drinks are being served. ANTHONY is on a post-performance high.

ANTHONY. Was I good?

PHILIP. You weren't bad at all.

ANTHONY. I'm used to extravagant flattery. Was I brilliant?

PHILIP. Just good.

ANTHONY. I might have known. A bucket of cold water. Ah. Excuse me a moment. Someone I must talk to. You'll be all right, won't you?

PHILIP. I'll be fine.

ANTHONY *dashes off.* PHILIP *is marooned for a bit. A lot of noise. People are talking all round him. Hold this for a little and then a voice cuts through.*

LAURA. You poor man. You look terribly lost. Are you a freshman?

PHILIP. That's right.

LAURA. I'm afraid I make a point of talking to strange men. Otherwise I never meet them. Were you listening to the debate?

PHILIP (*a smile*). A friend of mine was speaking.

LAURA. Oh? Who?

PHILIP. Anthony Moore.

LAURA (*laugh*). God, it would be, wouldn't it? Are you Philip Tremayne?

PHILIP. I'm afraid so.

LAURA. I'm Laura Kennedy. And why are you afraid so? All these men, apologising for themselves. It makes no sense.

PHILIP. What's he said about me?

LAURA. Oh, everything. He seems to admire you most of all for captaining the cricket Eleven. He says you're his good angel.

PHILIP. I had no idea.

LAURA. I bet you had. Modesty never fools me. You're not modest, are you?

PHILIP. No, probably not.

LAURA. Good. We'll get along fine. I gather you write.

PHILIP. I mess about.

LAURA. You're doing it again. You don't mess about. You've actually had a few things published.

PHILIP. Two things.

LAURA. Well, come on, it's impressive.

PHILIP. No, it's not. Neither of them was long. Two very short short stories.

LAURA. I call that impressive.

PHILIP. Have you read them?

LAURA. No. Why? Are they actually frightful?

PHILIP. Not frightful, competent. I've got a lot to learn. What do you do?

LAURA. I do lots of things. If you mean, what am I reading, I'm reading Greats. I know a lot about Herodotus.

PHILIP. That sounds intimidating.

LAURA. It is rather.

PHILIP. Anthony tells me you're the cleverest woman in your year.

LAURA. Well, there aren't all that many of us. Which makes Oxford rather a dangerous sort of place. But he's probably right. Going on the evidence to hand. Or at least I hope so. He's brilliant. He's going to be a don.

PHILIP. I didn't know that.

LAURA. It's the obvious thing for him to do. His tutor is C.S. Lewis and I gather it's all worked out. You do know who C.S. Lewis is?

PHILIP (*smile*). Yes.

LAURA. The view is that in his case finals is a foregone conclusion.

PHILIP (*smile*). I can't imagine Anthony messing up an exam. But I've always thought he wanted to go to London.

LAURA. Oh, he will. He'll be that sort of don. He'll broadcast and dine with people and then he'll get the train back here. Good heavens! You haven't got a drink. Don't stand here talking to me. Go and get one. It must be awful being sober with all the rest of us a little sozzled. Go on. I'll have a glass of white wine.

PHILIP. Right.

He turns and bumps straight into ANTHONY *who is heading over to join them.*

ANTHONY. You've met I see.

LAURA. We seem to have done.

PHILIP. I'm fetching Laura some refreshment.

ANTHONY. Good man.

> ANTHONY *talks to* LAURA *for a moment.* PHILIP *is in earshot.*

How was it?

LAURA. So-so, for you. That joke's been made before.

ANTHONY. It's still a good joke.

LAURA. Yes, but it's been made before.

> PHILIP *returns with the wine. He smiles.*

PHILIP. There's only red, I'm afraid.

LAURA. That won't do.

PHILIP. Fine by me. I'll have it.

LAURA (*to* ANTHONY). Your chum has no taste.

ANTHONY. He has, actually. And I dislike the word 'chum'.

LAURA. I need a cigarette.

ANTHONY. Don't look at me. They give me asthma.

PHILIP (*offering*). Here.

LAURA. Thank you. You're a sportsman and you smoke?

PHILIP. They do exist.

LAURA. Anthony says there's nothing more gross than a woman who smokes.

ANTHONY. Except a woman who gets drunk.

LAURA. There's this list of things I'm not allowed to do. I have to be constantly on my guard. A woman in an ocean of men.

PHILIP. It sounds all right to me.

LAURA. That's because you're a man.

ANTHONY. Come on.

LAURA. Oh, are we going somewhere?

ANTHONY. I've had enough of this.

LAURA. The night's still young.

ANTHONY. No it's not.

LAURA (*smile*). I'm sorry Philip. I'm being physically dragged away from you.

PHILIP (*smiling too*). He's always been possessive.

LAURA. I bet. So long.

PHILIP. Goodnight.

ANTHONY. Goodnight, Philip.

PHILIP. Have fun.

And he leaves as well. Down a staircase, out into the street. A cold, clear night. His footsteps echo as he runs.

PHILIP (*voice over*). It was later than I had realised and rather cold. I knew that if I didn't run I'd be locked out for the night.

He arrives breathless at the college gate where the PORTER *is locking up.*

PORTER (*smile*). I lock up regular as a rule, sir, but I don't suppose making an exception this once will do any harm.

PHILIP. Thanks, Reg. It's very good of you. (*Smile.*) I'm afraid I've been to a rather wonderful party. A very attractive young woman.

PORTER. Well, don't try to bring her over the wall, sir. We never fall for that.

PHILIP. Oh, I think I can be a bit more subtle.

PORTER. I'm sure you can, sir. Goodnight.

PHILIP. Goodnight, Reg. And thank you.

We lose this. We're in a small, rather expensive Oxford restaurant.

ANTHONY *is flushed and exuberant. He has probably never been so happy.*

ANTHONY. I know. I can't really believe it myself. I must seem like the least likely person. I'd have thought she'd have wanted someone very handsome and debonair but . . . well, it doesn't seem to matter. (*A moment.*) You've never had any trouble with women, have you?

PHILIP. Oh, I don't know. They seem to like me to begin with.

ANTHONY. The odd thing is, I hardly know Laura, really. I never feel particularly at ease when I'm with her. It's not like talking to you. And yet I feel so strongly. I think . . . this sounds ridiculously premature . . . but I think I want to marry her. (*A moment.*) I'm having a wonderful time, Philip, I really am. God knows what things are going to be like after this.

We lose this at once. We're in PHILIP's *college rooms. He's having tea with* LAURA.

PHILIP (*voice over*). A week or so later Laura sought me out. She seemed to be in some kind of trouble.

Into this immediately.

LAURA. We met at a seminar. I was reading a paper on the classical

influence on Augustan literature. It's a sort of hobby of mine.
I thought I was doing rather well. And then, suddenly, there was
this ferocious man arguing me into the ground. So when he
apologised and asked me to have tea I simply didn't dare to say no.

PHILIP. He can be intimidating, I know.

LAURA. Of course you know him much better than I do. That's why
I'm here. And we don't know each other all that well except for
. . . . I have this idea that he's mildly unhinged. I worry about what
might happen if things went wrong. I do have such respect for
him. But I feel tied down. And I don't think I should feel that.
I resent it rather. I have this demon in me, you know the feeling.

PHILIP. I know it well.

LAURA. What do you advise?

PHILIP. I don't know. (*Smile.*) Follow your nose, maybe.

LAURA. Yes, that seems very sane.

At once we lose this. We are briefly in a theatre: Gilbert and Sullivan.

PHILIP (*voice over*). That night I took her to the theatre. The Gilbert
and Sullivan Society were staging *Iolanthe*. And then I took her to
dinner and then she came back with me to my rooms.

LAURA *and* PHILIP *in bed. We're very close to them. They are both near
laughter.*

LAURA. Oh, Lord, Philip, what are we going to tell him?

PHILIP. These things happen. He'll have to learn.

LAURA. I can't bear the idea of hurting him.

PHILIP. Not much can be done about that now. (*Smile.*) I did know
he hadn't slept with you.

LAURA. Oh, how did you know that?

PHILIP. You don't fidget around like that with a woman you've
slept with.

LAURA. I suppose not.

PHILIP. He had no God-given right to you.

LAURA. No.

PHILIP. You don't rescind the right to choose simply because
someone asks you out. Oh, I know it'll upset him. I feel bad
about that too. But this is what happens. He can't . . . be
protected forever.

We lose this. PHILIP *narrates briefly. Very quiet.*

PHILIP (*voice over*). Two evenings later, he came round, very drunk,
and stood swaying in my doorway.

Into this immediately.

ANTHONY *is near hysterical.*

ANTHONY. How could you? (*Scream.*) How could you? I trusted you. I trusted you utterly.

PHILIP. Anthony, listen, please . . . .

ANTHONY. No, no. No. You listen. You listen. You could have had any woman you wanted, anyone in the world, you could have done what you liked with anyone, you could have crossed the globe and had anyone, anyone at all, anyone you wanted, anyone except Laura, you know that, you know that perfectly well, I know damn well you know it, but because it was Laura, because she was going out with me, because she was mine, you wanted her, you wanted to see if you could do it. I KNOW YOU!

PHILIP. That's not true.

ANTHONY. Oh, yes it bloody well is. You wanted to compete. You've wanted to for years. There are plenty of things you can do but you want to do what I can do as well. And you never will. And you never will because you're not as clever. You haven't my talent.

PHILIP. I know.

ANTHONY. You've killed me. Do you realise that? My life is in ruins. I'll never be happy again. I trusted you and you've KILLED ME!

PHILIP. Look. Please . . . .

ANTHONY. I suppose I can't ask you, for friendship's sake, just to leave her. Leave her and let me do the rest. No, of course I bloody well can't. I can't ask you for anything. You're worthless, Philip. You're the most worthless God-forsaken bloody awful person I've ever known.

And, as PHILIP *narrates, we lose this.* ANTHONY *goes out, slamming the door.*

PHILIP (*voice over*). And then he went. He never spoke to me again.

An interior acoustic. PHILIP *is at home with his* FATHER, *who is very angry and disquietingly calm.*

PHILIP. I'm as upset as he is, Pa.

FATHER. Don't be ridiculous. How could you possibly be? Do you expect me to be objective? I've known Anthony since he was eight. It seems to me that you've done an appalling thing. I've tried to raise you as a considerate, thoughtful and honest young man and I have failed utterly.

PHILIP. I have feelings, you know. I can't simply put them to one side.

FATHER. You may not credit this but there are certain things that, in friendship, a man simply does not do to another man. And what you've done is one of them. Don't ask me to salve your conscience. I hoped for better and I've been bitterly disappointed. What does any father say to a son like you?

And we lose this. An intimate acoustic. PHILIP *and* LAURA *together. A moment.*

LAURA. I keep thinking of him. I think of him more than I can tell you.

PHILIP. Oh, Laura.

LAURA. I should never have left him.

PHILIP. No one forced you. For Christ's sake, no one even made it difficult.

LAURA. You think it was easy?

PHILIP. I don't think it was difficult.

LAURA. It hurt him abominably. I knew it would when I did it.

PHILIP. So did I. Look. These things happen between people.

LAURA. Yes, but they shouldn't.

PHILIP. Don't be naive.

He's angry. He gets out of bed, sits thinking for a moment.

If you think that, then go. If it'll make your conscience easier. You talk as if I was the only one to blame. That's nonsense and you know it. So if you think he's the genius you say he is and you're missing out, then go. If you think I'm mediocre and dull and talentless, then for God's sake grab your things and go. I never pretended to be like him. He was simply my friend. I wish I'd never met him. So if you think you've backed the wrong horse, if you think you've destroyed his art or genius or whatever it is, then pack up now and go. The sooner the better.

A moment before we lose this. Then PHILIP *narrates.*

PHILIP (*voice over*). And, of course, she did. I heard later that she'd gone back to Anthony. Apparently there had been some stormy reconciliation and, when they gave him a fellowship, he married her. I wasn't invited to the wedding but, shortly afterwards, Laura sent me a sweet, rather generous letter. She asked me to forgive her. She felt she'd let me down. In the next year or two I gathered that she hadn't been very faithful. There were terrible quarrels, so their friends said, and, in an effort to sort things out, Anthony bought a small cottage in Dorset where they spent the vacations. By then I was living in London and, from time to time, Laura would come up to town to shop.

An interior acoustic. PHILIP's *little flat.* LAURA *has just arrived, a little breathless. He helps her off with her coat.*

LAURA. Thanks, Philip. It's impertinent of me to barge in like this and just assume we're still friends.

PHILIP. I think we're still friends. It's lovely to see you.

LAURA. I thought you could only tell me to go away again.

PHILIP. You're wearing an awful lot of clothes.

LAURA. It's the middle of October.

PHILIP. Does Anthony know you're here?

LAURA. No. I had some shopping to do. I had to get up to town. I think I'm a city girl deep down. I can't stand that tiny little farmhouse. Nothing all day but the sheep from across the field and Anthony's typewriter.

PHILIP. You should have been an air hostess.

LAURA (*smile*). Yes, I thought you'd say something like that. He's very kind. I don't think he's ever done a cruel thing in his life. But, oh, God, I do get tired of never seeing anyone.

PHILIP. You look terrific.

They sit down. LAURA *puts her shopping down.*

A drink?

She looks at him.

LAURA. I've come here to be comforted, Philip. I know you think I treated you badly. And I do love Anthony. I should probably never have got involved with either of you. It breaks my heart what happened. I'm not very happy, as you can probably tell.

PHILIP. Laura, I . . . .

LAURA. I won't say anything to Anthony. God, do you honestly think he'd mind? He knows its the price of peace. Otherwise we'll all go mad. And I do know now to keep very quiet. I've learnt so much from him but . . . I long sometimes for the ordinary. Ordinary, un-neurotic, healthy people who lead happy, healthy lives.

We lose this. Music plays. As PHILIP *narrates we are on the platform at Paddington.*

PHILIP (*voice over*). I put her on the train two hours later.

Into this immediately. LAURA's *train is about to pull out. The guard's whistle blows.*

LAURA. So long, Philip.

PHILIP. Goodbye, Laura.

LAURA. Be good.

PHILIP. I will.

And she goes. Music plays as PHILIP *narrates.*

PHILIP (*voice over*). What happened after that was reconstructed with some difficulty. Laura apparently arrived back very late. Anthony seemed to have locked her out. At any rate, all her things, her clothes, everything she owned, was found piled up in the yard. They think she probably broke a window and climbed in and they think he simply picked her up and carried her out again. Then he took a shotgun, shoved her up against the gate, and shot her with it. Then he went into the house, reloaded it, put the barrel in his mouth and blew his head off.

At once we are in TOMKIN's *living-room. A wood fire burns. He's older, retired, rather frail now. But he's very pleased to be visited. His spirits, as always, are high.*

TOMKIN. It's jolly good of you to come and see me, Tremayne.

PHILIP (*smile*). I could hardly have driven straight past the door.

TOMKIN. I'm fighting fit but I'm not as agile as I once was. I need a new back, but there we are. It's just old age.

PHILIP. Do you still play golf?

TOMKIN. Oh, I wish I could. That boy who was in your form, John Stevenage, he used to be awfully nice and come down and give me a game. I always lost. I used to say, well, John, the boot's on the other foot now. Of course, when he was with me he was a mathematical idiot but I gather he's making a mint in the City.

PHILIP (*smile*). I've heard that too.

TOMKIN. Do you keep up with anyone at all?

PHILIP. I'm afraid not. I've been very lazy about it.

TOMKIN. Oh, life leads us in unexpected directions. We can't all keep up. That boy Moore, the one who you used to be so thick with, I gather he killed himself.

PHILIP (*quiet*). I did hear that.

TOMKIN. A dreadful waste. Over a woman I'm told. I can remember him very well. He wasn't a happy boy. And everyone expected great things of him. You used to see him quite a bit, didn't you?

PHILIP. That's right. I'm afraid we lost touch in the end. National Service and all that. I saw the paper, of course.

TOMKIN. A dreadful waste. He can't have been very happy. I suppose he may be happier now.

PHILIP. Yes, that's . . . I'm sure that's true.

He gets up, puts his tea cup aside, takes TOMKIN's *hand.*

PHILIP. I must be getting along, I'm afraid.

TOMKIN. Of course, of course. Don't let me keep you. But any time you're passing. It's open house. Old Boys all the time.

They go into the hall. PHILIP *puts on his coat.*

When are you off to Greece?

PHILIP. In about a week. It'll be nice to see some sun.

TOMKIN. Oh, I bet.

PHILIP. I'm afraid I find this country rather depressing. And I've always wanted to travel.

TOMKIN. You couldn't have picked a better place. That deep, dark sea. Do send me a card if you have a moment. I suppose they'll be working you pretty hard.

PHILIP (*smile*). I doubt that. I can't believe teaching a little English for the British Council will be all that arduous. But I want time to think. I'd like to write a book. I'm really just being paid for getting away.

He gets into his car, switches on the engine, leans out to say goodbye.

TOMKIN. Well, Tremayne. It's been jolly nice to see you again. Do drop by when you eventually get back.

PHILIP. I certainly will. Anyway. Thanks for the tea. And take care, sir.

TOMKIN. Oh, I'll do that. Goodbye, Tremayne.

PHILIP. Goodbye, sir.

And he drives off, accelerating away. PHILIP *narrates. Music.*

PHILIP (*voice over*). The dead live a long time within us, in what we feel and breathe and think. They disrupt and confound our lives. They are not gone, not old, so long as I am still alive. Awake at night I dream and cannot be still. In the dark I hug my memories close. Your health. Your very good health. Cheers.

And we lose this. Silence.

THE GINGERBREAD HOUSE

by Ken Whitmore

For Pat and Eric Pringle, true pals

Ken Whitmore comes from the Potteries and went straight from school on to the local newspaper. Twenty-five years ago, a young newshound in Leeds, he was reading *Franny and Zooey* at the bar of a pub when a stranger showed great interest in the book and invited him for a drink with his companion. The man was the young novelist Stan Barstow and his companion the young radio producer Alfred Bradley. Bradley said if Whitmore ever wrote a play he should send it to him. Whitmore waited a dozen years before doing so and since then Alfred has directed all of his many radio plays. Ken Whitmore has also written for the stage (his latest publication being *La Bolshie Vita*) and is the author of *Jump!*, a children's novel. He has written many short stories and was winner of the Times/Jonathan Cape children's story competition. He and his wife Rosalind live in Cumbria and have four children aged from 2 to 22.

The Gingerbread House was first broadcast on BBC Radio 4 on 18 December 1986. The cast was as follows:

RICHARD	Nigel Anthony
CYNTHIA	Bonnie Hurren
HARRY	Judy Bennett
KATE	Bernadette Windsor

Director: Alfred Bradley
Running time, as broadcast: 52 minutes, 6 seconds

Fade in the sounds of a house.
Two CHILDREN *are heard laughing upstairs.*
The front doorbell chimes.
A door opens upstairs.

RICHARD (*off, upstairs*). Oh, hell! Who's that?

  The CHILDREN *laugh. The front doorbell chimes.*

  (*Coming downstairs.*) Yes, I'm coming! (*Calling back.*) You get your clothes on. You'll be catching pneumonia.

  He opens the front door.

  Yes? I'm sorry to keep you. I was bathing the children.

CYNTHIA. Oh, what fun. I'm Cynthia.

RICHARD. Cynthia?

CYNTHIA. A friend of Mary's. Cynthia Blanchard. You must be Richard.

RICHARD. Yes.

CYNTHIA. Is Mary at home?

RICHARD. Oh. You haven't heard.

CYNTHIA. No. Heard what?

RICHARD. You'd better come in.

  The door closes.

  In here please.

  The sitting-room door opens.

  Sitting-room. If you can navigate round the toys. I won't keep you a moment. (*He moves back into the hall and shouts up the stairs.*) Harry! Katie! Have you got your pyjamas on? (*He comes back to the sitting-room.*) Sorry about that.

CYNTHIA. I seem to have caught you at a hectic moment.

RICHARD. No, no. So . . . you're a friend of Mary's.

CYNTHIA (*pauses to decipher his awkwardness*). Good heavens, has she left you?

RICHARD. Oh, no. Well, yes. The truth is she died – just under a year ago – a year ago next month.

CYNTHIA. Oh, no.

RICHARD. Yes.

CYNTHIA. I've been abroad. I didn't know. We *had* rather lost touch.

RICHARD. May the fifteenth. A Sunday. Cancer, of course.

CYNTHIA. Oh God.

RICHARD. Yes, that's what I said. She was only thirty-eight. Oh, here are the children. Harry – Kate – may I present – a friend of your mummy's. Mrs – ahh – I'm afraid your name's gone.

CYNTHIA. Cynthia Blanchard. Hello. What lovely pyjamas.

RICHARD. Well, say hello.

HARRY. Hello.

RICHARD. Kate, where's your tongue?

KATE. Hello.

CYNTHIA. And how old are you?

HARRY. Ten.

RICHARD. And little Kate is all of eight, aren't you darling? Harry, let me feel your hair. Oh, lord. And yours, too, baby. Dearie me, what are we going to do with you? Up you go and dry it properly. Go on. Shoo.

HARRY *and* KATE *run upstairs, laughing.*

CYNTHIA. They look exactly like Mary.

RICHARD. Yes.

CYNTHIA. Particularly the little girl.

RICHARD. Yes. I'm glad to say. Though it does have its painful moments. Sorry. I'm a very sentimental man.

CYNTHIA. You have something to be sentimental about.

RICHARD. We had too little time together. It was my silly fault.

CYNTHIA. I don't see how you can say that.

RICHARD. No, I mean we should have married sooner. Years sooner. I knew her for such a long time and never did anything about it. I'm a solicitor, you know, specialising in insurance claims. She was secretary to the senior partner. That was far too grand for me. Like marrying the king's daughter. Even so, I plucked up courage and asked her out to lunch one day. But I was tongue-tied. Felt terribly unworthy. And she, bless her heart, was an old-fashioned sort of girl. Wouldn't take the lead. I left it seven years before I asked her out again.

CYNTHIA. Good Lord.

RICHARD. It was the day I was made a partner. Took her out to dinner this time. Asked her to marry me while she was studying the menu. She looked up and said yes straight away. Told me she'd been in love with me all those seven years.

CYNTHIA. Good Lord.

RICHARD. Yes. Seven wasted years. We had young Harry almost at once. (*Pause.*) So you and she were friends.

CYNTHIA. School friends. We were once hauled up before the dreaded Miss Antrobus for fighting.

RICHARD. Oh, I believe she told me something about that. Something about a chipped tooth.

CYNTHIA. Yes, she chipped my tooth. Look.

RICHARD. Good Lord, did Mary do that?

CYNTHIA. With her fist. Well I asked for it.

RICHARD. Good Lord, she was such a peaceful little mouse. Never laid a finger on me.

CYNTHIA. Well, she did my tooth in. And then we became friends. I'm so dreadfully sorry. How wickedly wasteful.

RICHARD. It was, rather. (*Pause.*) Abroad, you say?

CYNTHIA. Yes, I'm a journalist. I've been in the States for the last two years. Africa before that. Scandinavia. I've got a contract with the *Guardian*. That's what brought me home. You might have seen some of my pieces.

RICHARD. No, I'm afraid we take the *Mail*. The children like the cartoons and the horoscopes.

CYNTHIA. The horoscopes?

RICHARD. Yes, why?

The CHILDREN *scream upstairs.*

CYNTHIA. Sorry, I can see you're on pins to see to the children.

RICHARD. No, they're only killing each other. Look, I'll just go and read them a story and I'll be with you in a couple of –

CYNTHIA. Excuse me. Do I smell something burning?

RICHARD. Gosh, yes, I've got a chop in the oven. My dinner.

CYNTHIA. You seem just a little harassed. Why don't I get your dinner?

RICHARD. Oh, no, I couldn't let you.

CYNTHIA. You go and see to the children. Take as long as you like. And I'll make you a very special dinner. I bet you haven't had a decent one for a long time.

RICHARD. Well . . .

CYNTHIA. Is there any wine in the house?

RICHARD. No, I haven't gone in for wine since Mary –

CYNTHIA. There's a shop on the corner. I'll go and get a bottle of Rioja.

RICHARD. I don't know why you're taking all this trouble.

CYNTHIA. Say I'm doing it for Mary.

Fade out.

Fade in the dining-room.

RICHARD. That's is the best meal I've eaten since . . . well, a long time.

CYNTHIA. We must do it again.

RICHARD. Do you really mean that?

CYNTHIA. I never say what I don't mean. Here, you might as well finish the wine.

RICHARD. No, no, you've hardly had a drop and my head isn't used to wine these days.

CYNTHIA. Here, it will do you good. It's already doing you good.

She pours wine.

RICHARD. I must go up and take a look at the children.

CYNTHIA. You did that five minutes ago.

RICHARD. Did I? Good Lord, I believe I did.

CYNTHIA. How do you cope, Richard?

RICHARD. How do I cope?

CYNTHIA. With all this – the children?

RICHARD. God knows. No, actually, it's simple. In the morning, drop them off at school. In the afternoon our daily comes in, Mrs Garnett, tidies around, picks them up from school, feeds them, puts me a meal in the oven, waits for me to arrive at 6.30, departs.

CYNTHIA. Weekends?

RICHARD. I have the little beggars all to myself.

CYNTHIA. What do you do with them?

RICHARD. Feed them, drag them round with me.

CYNTHIA. Where to?

RICHARD. Rugger matches mostly.

CYNTHIA. Rugger?

RICHARD. I'm a referee.

CYNTHIA. And what do they do while you're refereeing?

RICHARD. Cheer the ref. Everybody else boos the ref.

CYNTHIA. Don't they get bored?

RICHARD (*surprised*). They've never said so.

CYNTHIA. And cold?

RICHARD (*worried*). They don't complain. I suppose they're used to it. A hallowed family tradition. Mary brought them along from being toddlers. No, younger. They came in backpacks when they were babies.

CYNTHIA. That's Saturdays. What about Sundays?

RICHARD. The garden. Weeding and romping and sudden screaming rushes inside to see if the potatoes have boiled away or the meat's been burned. Somehow Sunday lunch consumes all of Sunday. Still washing up as the moon rises. Wouldn't miss it, though. They're worth it. Lucky to have them.

Pause.

CYNTHIA. It's a beautiful house. Beautiful furniture.

RICHARD. You're a beautiful woman.

CYNTHIA. You must have a very successful practice.

RICHARD. Oh, because of the house. No, this place belonged to my brother, who died. He was the successful one of the family but he went and died. Died before he lived, you might say, because he never married. Excuse me, I think I'm a little tight.

CYNTHIA. No, you're just relaxed.

RICHARD. Where do *you* live?

CYNTHIA. Muswell Hill. I share a microscopic flat with a mountainous girl violinist in the LSO.

RICHARD. Sounds uncomfortable.

CYNTHIA. It's a bit difficult to get any writing done.

RICHARD. I've been lucky with property. We've a cottage in the Yorkshire Dales, too. We call it our little gingerbread house. That was handed me on a plate, too. My father bought it for his

retirement but he and mother both died. People have a silly habit
of dying in our family and I'm the one who always gets left
behind. Some people might call it luck but it gets awfully lonely.
Sorry, getting maudlin and sentimental.

CYNTHIA. Drink up your wine.

RICHARD. Well: to many meetings.

CYNTHIA. Many meetings. And now you can kiss me.

RICHARD. Can I really?

CYNTHIA. Don't you want to?

RICHARD. I've been wanting to for about – (*Looking at his watch.*) –
three quarters of an hour.

CYNTHIA. Then do it. (*They share a long kiss.*) Now upstairs.

RICHARD. Upstairs?

CYNTHIA. To bed.

RICHARD. Why, are you leaving?

CYNTHIA. I mean take me to bed.

RICHARD. I say, you're so very direct.

CYNTHIA. I'm just straightforward. I'm not one to wait seven years.
Come.

RICHARD. But the children.

CYNTHIA. The children are asleep.

RICHARD. But wait . . . do you mean in Mary's bed?

CYNTHIA. Richard, it's any old bed. Now come. Come, Richard . . .

   Fade out.

   Fade in a newspaper office with a typewriter in the background.

RICHARD (*distort*). Hello, it's Richard.

CYNTHIA. Richard?

RICHARD. Yes.

CYNTHIA. I'm sorry, Richard who?

RICHARD. Richard Brimley.

CYNTHIA. Oh yes?

RICHARD. When can we meet again? (*Pause.*) Are you still
there?

CYNTHIA. Yes. Yes, I'm still here.

RICHARD. When could we meet?

CYNTHIA. What for?

RICHARD. What for?

CYNTHIA. I'm rather busy at the moment, Richard. I have an article to finish.

RICHARD. Ah. Could we have lunch, perhaps?

CYNTHIA. Richard, I . . . (*Long pause.*)

RICHARD. Yes?

CYNTHIA. I'm really tremendously tied up at the moment . . . deadlines . . . you know?

RICHARD. Please say yes.

CYNTHIA. Richard . . . .

RICHARD. It means an awful lot to me. Please say yes.

   Pause.

CYNTHIA. Yes.

RICHARD. Ah.

CYNTHIA. All right, Richard.

RICHARD. Lunch?

CYNTHIA. All right. Where do you suggest?

   Fade out.

   Fade in a restaurant.

CYNTHIA. Thank you, Richard, that was perfect.

RICHARD. Yes, we must come here again, it was recommended by a client of mine, really excellent.

CYNTHIA. Richard.

RICHARD. Yes?

CYNTHIA. I don't think that would be a good idea.

RICHARD. Sorry?

CYNTHIA. I don't want to hurt your feelings but I don't think there's much future in this.

RICHARD. Oh. In us? (*Pause.*) But I don't understand. We made – (*Lowering his voice.*) we made love together.

CYNTHIA. So we did.

RICHARD. I don't understand. Doesn't that mean anything?

CYNTHIA. Not these days. Where have you been?

RICHARD. I suppose I must have been . . . living in another world. But I still can't understand why you let –

CYNTHIA. Because you'd taken such a battering. I'm a sucker for lost causes. It was the picture of you rushing in from the garden and finding the joint was a funeral pyre. And still washing up as the moon rose. It touches the stoniest heart – which mine is, by the way.

RICHARD. Am I a lost cause? Good grief.

CYNTHIA. No, you're a perfect gent of a sort I don't meet very often. Unfortunately it wouldn't work.

RICHARD. It could do.

CYNTHIA. You've got a nice little family. Don't destroy it. I'd be an intruder. I'm from another world, literally. I'm at the opposite pole from Mary. I fly off the handle.

RICHARD. But Cynthia –

CYNTHIA. Listen, I'm bossy. I'd interfere. I have very strong ideas about how the universe should run. I'm the candid friend who punctures illusions. I've left a trail of collapsed egos around the world.

RICHARD. I don't care.

CYNTHIA. No, it wouldn't do.

RICHARD. It would, I'm sure it would!

CYNTHIA. Richard, I don't want to get sucked in. It would be unfair. It would be dangerous.

RICHARD. Dangerous? How?

CYNTHIA. Just a feeling I have.

RICHARD. You're wrong. You're just what I need.

CYNTHIA. But do I need you?

RICHARD. Oh.

CYNTHIA. An ageing gent with two kids nearing the awkward age?

RICHARD. What an idiot. I never thought of that.

CYNTHIA. No.

RICHARD. No. (*Pause.*) Oh, I forgot to give you this.

CYNTHIA. What, for me?

RICHARD. Little present.

CYNTHIA. You shouldn't have done. Shall I open it now?

RICHARD. Yes.

    She unwraps chocolates.

CYNTHIA (*laughing*). Chocolates! Oh, no!

RICHARD. What's the matter? Don't you like chocolates?

CYNTHIA. What, you haven't noticed my figure? You can't see I'm fighting to lose weight?

RICHARD. You're not, surely?

CYNTHIA. You didn't notice what I had for lunch?

RICHARD. Eh?

CYNTHIA. The starvation rations?

RICHARD. No. Good heavens.

CYNTHIA. You're so unobservant. You're so innocent.

RICHARD. My mind must have been elsewhere. But your figure's perfect. What nonsense.

CYNTHIA. Next time flowers – or, if you're feeling flush, scent.

RICHARD. Next time?

CYNTHIA. Yes, next time. I give in. But please don't say I didn't warn you.

Fade out.

Fade in the hall of the house.
A flap on.

RICHARD. Well have you looked in the airing cupboard?

KATE. I tell you I've looked in the airing cupboard.

RICHARD. Well look again.

KATE. I have looked again.

RICHARD (*calling*). Any luck, Harry?

HARRY (*coming downstairs*). No luck up there. I've hunted all over.

RICHARD. How about my wardrobe?

HARRY. Yes, I looked.

RICHARD. My big chest of drawers.

HARRY. Yes, no joy.

RICHARD. The blanket chest.

KATE. I turned the blanket chest out. No rugger togs, but you know what I did find? My recorder. Mummy must have put it away in there before . . .

RICHARD. Yes.

Pause.

HARRY. Dad, I think I'll come to the rugger match with *you*.

RICHARD. No, Harry.

HARRY. Oh, Daddy.

RICHARD. That would be impolite.

HARRY. OK. Sorry.

RICHARD. Have you looked in Mummy's room?

HARRY. Yes, are you sure you haven't taken them out to the car?

RICHARD. No, I just went out to look. How about the cupboard under the stairs? The laundry basket?

KATE. We've looked! We've looked everywhere!

HARRY. The mystery of the missing rugger kit.

He and KATE *laugh.*

RICHARD. This is maddening. How can they simply vanish from the face of the earth?

KATE. The case of the disappearing drawers!

She and HARRY *roar.*

RICHARD. Look, it's no joke.

The doorbell rings.

RICHARD. Calm down. It's Cynthia. She'll think you're a couple of chattering chimpanzees.

The KIDS *giggle and imitate chimps.*

The door opens.

RICHARD. Cynthia, come in, well, you're looking –

CYNTHIA. Hello, Richard.

The door closes.

CYNTHIA. Kate. Harry.

KIDS (*subdued*). Hello.

Pause – the KIDS *are a bit hostile and awkward.*

RICHARD. Yes. Well then. Lovely day for the zoo. You're looking . . . splendid. Quite a glow in your cheeks. Children – you know Cynthia. (*Pause.*) There's a bag of doughnuts in the kitchen – for the elephants. Bad news though.

CYNTHIA. Oh?

RICHARD. Yes, there's a bit of a crisis. I don't know where Mrs Garnett's gone and hidden my rugger togs.

CYNTHIA. Dreadful. Alert Interpol.

Pause – the joke falls flat.

RICHARD. We've been looking for them. I'll tell you what, children, you go and show Cynthia the house. She's never seen it by daylight. And I'll have a methodical search. All right, Cynthia?

CYNTHIA. Yes, I'd love to see the house.

RICHARD. All right, Kate, what are you waiting for? You lead the way.

KATE. Upstairs?

RICHARD. Yes.

KATE. What, Mummy's room as well?

RICHARD. Yes.

KATE. Mummy doesn't like strangers staring at her things.

RICHARD. Katie, what will Cynthia think? Cynthia isn't a stranger.

CYNTHIA. It's all right Richard. Some other time.

RICHARD. No, no, no. Up you go. Go on. And I'll look for those rugger things . . . .

Crossfade to an upstairs passage.

KATE. Just along here. Here we are. This is Mummy and Daddy's bedroom.

The bedroom door opens.

KATE. There.

CYNTHIA. Pretty.

KATE. That's Mummy and Daddy's bed. Mummy sleeps on that side. (*Pause.*) Now we'll go and see Mummy's room.

CYNTHIA. There's really no need.

KATE. Yes, Daddy said so. This way.

They move.

Here we are. Come in. This is where she does all her sewing.

CYNTHIA. That's a very old sewing machine.

KATE. Yes, it belonged to Grandma.

CYNTHIA. Are these your mummy's dolls?

KATE. Yes, from when she was a little girl.

CYNTHIA. Oh, I should be on this photograph somewhere. Yes, look, at the back with terrible straight hair.

HARRY. Mummy's sitting in the middle of the front row.

CYNTHIA. So she is.

HARRY Holding the shield.

CYNTHIA. Yes, I remember that day.

KATE. Were you good friends?

CYNTHIA. Of course.

KATE. Did you like David Deerwood?

CYNTHIA. David Deerwood?

KATE. He was Mummy's sweetheart at school. He was the gardener's son.

CYNTHIA. David Deerwood? I'm afraid he was rather dishonest.

KATE (*puzzled*). I don't think so.

CYNTHIA. Yes, he was rather two-faced. I'm sure your mother never had anything to do with a boy like that.

KATE (*puzzled*). Well, she did.

CYNTHIA. She must have been pulling your leg.

HARRY. Mummy was the head girl. That's why she's holding the shield.

CYNTHIA. Yes, I know, dear.

HARRY. And captain of hockey. And editor of the school magazine.

CYNTHIA. Yes, I know, dear. I was there. What a great pity she didn't follow it all up.

RICHARD (*entering*). Hello. Who didn't follow *what* up?

CYNTHIA. Hello, Richard. I was just wondering why Mary took such a deep dive into domesticity.

RICHARD. A deep dive? I think she just felt fulfilled – by family life. (*Pause.*) They were in the airing cupboard all the time. Somebody hadn't looked properly.

Fade out.

Fade in the house.
The doorbell rings. Pause. The door opens.

RICHARD. Thank God. Where in heaven have you been?

KATE. Daddy, Daddy, Daddy!

CYNTHIA. Sorry we're late, darling, I tried to ring.

RICHARD. I've been on the brink of a breakdown.

The door closes.

You're so late.

CYNTHIA. I thought they could stay up for once.

RICHARD. Yes, but it's so late. My heart was in my mouth. Couldn't you have rung?

CYNTHIA. I tried, but either the boxes were out of order or –

RICHARD. Katie, let me take that coat off. Oh, look at her poor pale little face.

HARRY. Daddy, we went to the War Museum.

RICHARD. The War Museum? What, after you'd been to the zoo?

CYNTHIA. I wasn't up to the zoo today somehow.

RICHARD. Oh?

CYNTHIA. And then we went to the *Observer* and saw the paper being put to bed. I have this friend on the features desk, Fulton Calthorpe, he showed them everything, he was so sweet, wasn't he children? And we all had fish and chips in the composing room.

RICHARD. Fish and chips? What, the children?

HARRY. We had ice cream, Daddy.

RICHARD. Really? After the fish and chips?

CYNTHIA. No, that was this afternoon, after the War Museum.

RICHARD. I thought you were going to the zoo.

CYNTHIA. I couldn't face the zoo.

RICHARD. You took the doughnuts for the elephants.

CYNTHIA. We gave them to the pigeons at Westminster Cathedral.

KATE (*wailing*). I wanted the elephants.

CYNTHIA. Oh, dear, it took ages to steer her off that and you've brought it all back.

KATE. I wanted the elephants!

CYNTHIA. Katie, look what I've got for you. Your Mars Bar.

HARRY. I wanted the elephants as well.

CYNTHIA. Yes, there's a Mars Bar for you, too, Harry. There you are, dear.

RICHARD. What's all this? Fish and chips, ice cream, Mars Bars? Really, Cynthia.

CYNTHIA. What's the matter?

RICHARD. Mary never – I mean we didn't allow – I mean stuff like that's not good for them. Their teeth.

CYNTHIA. Oh tosh. Bosh. They're only young once, Richard.

RICHARD. Yes, but some things are absolutely poison, surely. Run up and get into your pyjamas. And *scrub* those teeth.

CYNTHIA. Look at you, poisoning yourself with that filthy pipe.

The CHILDREN *run giggling upstairs.*

RICHARD (*worriedly to himself*). Well, at least, it seems to have been a success.

Fade out.

Fade in the bedroom.
RICHARD *and* CYNTHIA *are breathing hard after making love.*

RICHARD. I'm out of trim, out of kilter, my heart will go.

CYNTHIA. No, you were wonderful.

RICHARD. I'm perfectly shattered.

CYNTHIA. You shattered me perfectly – into a million lovely pieces.

RICHARD. It was all right, wasn't it?

CYNTHIA. Perfect.

RICHARD. There's only one thing.

CYNTHIA. Oh yes?

RICHARD. Do you have to make all that noise?

CYNTHIA. What?

RICHARD. Do you have to scream so? The children.

CYNTHIA. They've been asleep for hours. Even if they're not, children have been hearing that since the beginning of time.

RICHARD. Not my children. Mary never – I'm sorry.

CYNTHIA. No, go on.

RICHARD. Mary never uttered a sound.

CYNTHIA. Neither do you. I don't know how you hold it in. And yet you're so good. (*Giggling.*) Think what you'd be like if you let it out. Would you like to try again?

RICHARD. What?

CYNTHIA. And lose control this time?

RICHARD. I'd love to. But not tonight. Please.

CYNTHIA. Look, we'll try something different.

RICHARD. Good God, wasn't *that* different?

CYNTHIA. My goodness, Richard, that was practically basic. Look, we'll try this.

Fade out.

Fade in the dining-room.
The CHILDREN *are giggling at the table.*

RICHARD. Now, children, children – this is a very special dinner. That's why you're staying up late. We've something very special to tell you. Cynthia and Daddy were married today. So Cynthia is your new . . . Cynthia is going to look after you from now on just like – erm –

CYNTHIA (*to his rescue*). And I want you both to call me Cynthia, not Mummy or Auntie or any of that nonsense. Technically I'm what is known as a stepmother, but I'd hate to be called stepmother because of all the adverse colouring that word's taken on through the stereotyping effect of fairy-stories down the ages. Oh, dear, simple language, simple language. I mean stepmothers are painted as pure horrors and I hope I won't be. There. Cynthia has said her piece.

RICHARD. Yes. And now, Katie, would you please say Grace?

KATE (*after clearing her throat*). Bless, O Lord, this food we take; bless us, too, for Jesu's sake.

CYNTHIA. Oh, shit!

KATE. Amen.

CYNTHIA. Sorry, I knocked the salt over.

KATE. Over your shoulder!

HARRY. Throw it over your shoulder!

RICHARD. Cynthia.

CYNTHIA. Yes?

RICHARD. We don't go in for words like that at this table.

CYNTHIA (*laughing it off*). What? I didn't know you objected to a bit of strong language.

RICHARD. I call it weak language.

KATE. Cynthia, you've got to throw salt over your shoulder.

CYNTHIA. No, dear, that's just a stupid superstition and it puts up our salt bills and makes extra work for Mrs Garnett.

KATE. But Mummy says you –

CYNTHIA. Katie. Your mother is dead. Dead. Do you understand? Your mother is dead. (*Pause.*) No, love, no need to get down. Oh, dear, what have I done? Where are you going, Katie?

RICHARD. Kate!

The door opens and closes.

CYNTHIA. Oh, God, what have I done?

RICHARD. Harry, just slip out and see she's all right, there's a good lad.

The door opens and closes for HARRY.

CYNTHIA. I mean, surely she knows her mother's dead.

RICHARD. I don't think it's been put to her quite so bluntly before.

CYNTHIA. But surely she went to the funeral.

RICHARD. Of course not. She was only seven years old.

CYNTHIA. Did Harry go?

RICHARD. Of course not.

CYNTHIA. But they should have done. Otherwise it's like a wound that never heals. Where on earth do they think she is?

RICHARD. In Heaven.

CYNTHIA. Heaven? You can't fob them off with these fairy-stories. It's unfair. Do you hear me? Those children have got to mourn properly and get it out of their system. I need a glass of wine.

Wine poured.

Richard, do we have to have grace?

RICHARD. Grace?

CYNTHIA. Grace before meals. It makes me squirm. That's why I knocked the salt over.

RICHARD. On purpose?

CYNTHIA. It's so Winnie the Pooh. It's so Christopher Robin.

RICHARD. What's wrong with Winnie the Pooh?

CYNTHIA. It's so smug, so suburban, so middle-class.

RICHARD. Good God, is it? The children love it.

CYNTHIA. You mean you've got the books? In the house?

RICHARD. All of them.

CYNTHIA. Good God.

She starts to laugh hysterically.

Fade out.

Fade in.
Door chimes.

RICHARD. Coming, coming.

The door opens.

RICHARD. At last. Only two hours late. Where did you get to this time?

HARRY. Hi, Dad.

KATE. Hello, Daddy.

CYNTHIA. Well let us in. It's drizzling out here.

The door closes.

RICHARD. Well, did you finally get to the zoo this time?

CYNTHIA. Oh, yes, we got to the *zoo* all right.

HARRY. No we didn't.

KATE. I didn't like it. I don't want to go there again.

RICHARD. Get those coats off. They're damp. Well, *did* you get to the zoo or didn't you? There seems to be some disagreement.

CYNTHIA. Yes, we got to a zoo called Greenham Common.

RICHARD. Greenham Common?

CYNTHIA. Where all the dangerous animals are kept in cages with their dangerous toys.

Pause.

RICHARD. You took these babies to Greenham Common?

CYNTHIA. Okay, shoot me down, but they've got to know what it's all about, Richard.

Pause.

RICHARD. Have you eaten?

CYNTHIA. We found a good transport café outside Reading.

RICHARD. Fish and chips?

CYNTHIA. Sausage and chips.

RICHARD. I see.

HARRY. Dad, you should really have been there. The police charged with their batons. It was amazing.

KATE. Everybody was screaming. I didn't like it. I hated it.

CYNTHIA. Now then, Katie.

KATE. I don't want to go to that zoo again.

CYNTHIA. They were in no danger, Richard. I kept well back.

KATE. I didn't like it when Cynthia was screaming.

RICHARD. Yes, all right, dear. You won't have to go there again. Now if you've eaten you'd better go up and get ready for bed. It's past your bedtime.

KATE. Will you come up and tell us a story?

RICHARD. Yes, when you're ready.

Pause while the KIDS *go.*

(*To* CYNTHIA:) Will you come in here?

CYNTHIA. I must go and dry my hair.

RICHARD. Come in here.

CYNTHIA. Very well.

They move from the hall.

RICHARD. Close the door.

The door closes.

CYNTHIA. I'm not on the defensive, if that's what you think.

RICHARD. No?

CYNTHIA. They had to see it, Richard. It's their lives. It's the reality. It's their future. It isn't fairy-tales. It isn't zoos. It's what's happening now – in England. It's time they grew up.

RICHARD. They seem to have aged quite a lot. Katie suddenly looked as old as you. What right had you? What right?

CYNTHIA. Listen, Richard, the world isn't Winnie the Pooh's Four Acre Wood. It isn't Christopher Robin. It isn't a dream world. It's a world of missiles and starvation and terrorists. It's a world of torture and assassination and napalm.

RICHARD. Do you think they won't get that news soon enough? Just leave them alone. I don't know – you come here – you make wholesale changes in the house – you tear Mary's room to pieces –

CYNTHIA. Naturally. A second wife naturally wants to make over the house in her own way.

RICHARD. You can't make over Harry and Kate.

CYNTHIA. I can have a jolly good try.

RICHARD. They're perfectly all right as they are.

CYNTHIA. No they aren't. They wear coats when all the other children are wearing anoraks.

RICHARD. Coats? Now even their coats are wrong. Mary obviously didn't get a single thing right.

CYNTHIA. Not a lot.

RICHARD. Oh, balls! Now there – look there – you've even started to degrade my speech.

CYNTHIA. No, I've started to liberate it. Go on, have a good curse, it'll do you good.

RICHARD. Damn you. Sometimes I can almost see why Mary walloped you. (*Pause.*) Are you after some sort of revenge, is that what all this is about? What *did* you and Mary fight over?

CYNTHIA. Sweets.

RICHARD. Sweets? Yes, it all starts to come back. That's right. She caught you stealing her jelly babies.

CYNTHIA. Jelly babies, Liquorice Allsorts, what's the difference?

RICHARD. She was a day girl. Loving parents she always went home to at night. Always came to school loaded with sweets, fruit. You were a boarder. Got no affection at home. They never sent you a parcel. I remember now. It was a story she used to worry about. One day she found you with her box of jelly babies. Didn't mind. She just didn't want you to eat them *all*. She was generous with her things. But you stood there guzzling them down, stuffing yourself. So she walloped you.

The door opens.
HARRY *clears his throat slightly.*

Yes, Freud would say you wanted to eat her babies. Is that it? Do you want to eat Harry and Kate?

CYNTHIA. Shh! The children.

RICHARD. Oh, hello.

CYNTHIA. Harry, Kate, hello, are you ready? Come on, let me take you up to bed.

KATE. No, please! She'll eat us up.

HARRY. Daddy! Don't let her!

CYNTHIA. But Kate – Harry –

The CHILDREN *scream and run upstairs.*

Fade out.

Fade in the bedroom.
RICHARD *turns over.*

RICHARD. Are you awake? Cynthia? Still awake?

CYNTHIA. Yes.

RICHARD. I'm sorry.

CYNTHIA. No, it was my silly fault. I'm going too fast. I'm so uncompromising. And you're such a wimp.

RICHARD. Wimp? I hate that word. It's just a spiteful label for most of the qualities I admire and try to live up to. Tolerance, sentiment, gentleness, reserve.

CYNTHIA. What word would you put in its place?

RICHARD. Gentleman.

CYNTHIA (*giggling*). Oh, you're so pompous. You adorable pompous wimp. I love you.

RICHARD. Cynthia –

CYNTHIA. Shut up. Just hold me. Hold me.

Fade in the CHILDREN's *bedroom.*

In the distance, screams and groans.

KATE. Harry, what's that? Harry!

HARRY. Yes, I know.

KATE. Listen.

HARRY. I can hear.

KATE. I'm frightened. Get in with me.

HARRY comes across and gets in her bed.

KATE. What's she doing? She's eating him, isn't she? She's eating Daddy.

HARRY. No. I don't know.

KATE. She is! And then it will be our turn.

HARRY. Hush. No.

Silence.

KATE. She's finished. Now it's our turn.

HARRY. No! No!

KATE (*screams repeatedly*). It's our turn! It's our turn!

HARRY. Quiet! Quiet. (*Pause.*) Somebody's coming.

KATE. No. Please.

The door opens.

RICHARD. Katie? Did you have a bad dream?

KATIE (*sobs uncontrollably*). Oh, Daddy! Daddy! Daddy!

Fade out.

Fade in the living-room.
The door opens.

CYNTHIA. Hello, Richard, children in bed?

The door closes.

RICHARD. Yes, hours ago. A man rang up.

CYNTHIA. For me?

RICHARD. Yes, he wanted to invite you to a gay symposium on women-only graveyards. Was he serious, do you think?

CYNTHIA. Oh, that would be Fulton Calthorpe.

RICHARD. Yes, that was the name. Was he being serious?

CYNTHIA. Fulton's always serious, why?

RICHARD. Women-only graveyards?

CYNTHIA. Yes, why not?

RICHARD. Oh, no reason at all, dear. Single-sex cemeteries. Yes, why not indeed?

CYNTHIA. On Saturday, Richard, I know I said I'd take the children to the Unicorn Theatre but I ran into Hilda Farmer tonight and she was in a hell of a flap, she wants me to take her battered wives.

RICHARD. Take them where?

CYNTHIA. Here, on Saturday afternoon, so I said yes.

RICHARD. Battered wives?

CYNTHIA. It's their weekly get-together.

RICHARD. What about the children?

CYNTHIA. They can stay here. In fact it might do Kate good to sit in on the meeting. She'll learn what goes on in the outside world.

RICHARD. Kate? Oh, no, I don't think so. Not Kate.

CYNTHIA. Richard, they won't have black eyes and bloodstained bandages.

RICHARD. Saturday? You know, it went clean out of my head. I'm taking them to see their Aunt Dorothy in Herne Bay.

CYNTHIA. Oh. Oh, well, there'll be other Saturdays.

RICHARD. What? We're having them here every Saturday?

Fade out.

Fade in the CHILDREN's *bedroom.*

CYNTHIA. Hello, children, all tucked up warm?

KATE. Yes.

CYNTHIA. Good. I'm going to tell you a little story. Shove up, Kate.

KATE. Where's Daddy?

CYNTHIA. Washing the dishes. Now I'm going to read you this *true* story, a real-life story. Out of this book.

HARRY. I wanted a ghost-story.

KATE. No, a fairy-story!

CYNTHIA. Fairy-stories are lies. That's why we say, when somebody tells a fib, don't tell fairy-stories.

KATE. No, that's not the same.

CYNTHIA. Yes it is. Now hush. Listen, this is far more interesting.

KATE. Has it got any pictures?

CYNTHIA. Of course.

KATE. Let me see. (*Pause.*) He's a black boy.

CYNTHIA. Yes. Now lie back and listen. 'Edward was a socially underprivileged boy of –'

KATE. What's socially underprimitive?

CYNTHIA. He was socially deprived.

KATE. What's that mean?

CYNTHIA. Poor.

KATE. Oh, good, he'll get rich, I know, bags and bags of gold.

CYNTHIA. Don't be so sure. 'Edward was a socially underprivileged boy of Jamaican descent –'

KATE. Uh?

CYNTHIA. '– living in the black ghetto of Lewisham. One day he was on his way to the comprehensive school when –'

KATE. Cynthia, what's a black gâteau?

HARRY. It's a cake.

CYNTHIA. No, no, Harry.

HARRY. Yes, it is. A black forest gâteau.

KATE. The boy was living in a cake? This is a silly story. I want a fairy-story.

HARRY. A ghost-story!

KATE. I want my Daddy.

HARRY. Do you know the shortest ghost-story in the world? The bald-headed man went to sleep in the haunted bedroom. He hung his wig on the bedpost and when he woke up in the morning it had turned white.

HARRY *and* KATE *are hooting with laughter.*

Fade out.

Fade in the sitting-room.

CYNTHIA. Richard, this ghosts and goblins thing has got to end. They're living in a dream world.

RICHARD. All right, what do you want to put in its place?

CYNTHIA. People are starving. There are four million unemployed. I want to teach them to identify with the dispossessed. I'm a rational being in a rational world.

RICHARD. Yes, but you see, children don't live in a rational world. You can't suddenly clap your hands and banish the world they've built up in their imagination. Anyway, why should you?

CYNTHIA. Because I'm a rational human being.

RICHARD. Well try to go one step at a time. You rush blindly on.

CYNTHIA. I am not blind. It's you that's blind. You and Mary kept those children in – God – in a Victorian belljar of fantasy and whimsy, of *Winnie the Pooh* and *Watership Down*.

RICHARD. *Watership Down*? I loathe *Watership Down*. Rabbits with social problems.

CYNTHIA. Really? That sounds interesting.

RICHARD. Oh, I'm sure you'd like it.

CYNTHIA. Don't try to sidetrack me.

RICHARD. I wasn't. What I'm trying to say is that a family . . . a family has its own mysteries, its own magical rites, its own secret code that an outsider couldn't crack in a thousand years, its own jokes that leave outsiders cold, its own rituals. And you interfere with all that at your own peril.

CYNTHIA. Well I'm interfering with fairy-stories. They're out.

RICHARD. Fairy-stories started at their mother's knee. They drank them in with her milk. It was the air they breathed. Their element. You can't blow that away overnight – disperse it and bring in the reign of socialist realism. Look, those kids are like two plants in a pot. They're deep in the soil, *her* soil. You can't suddenly uproot them, put them in another pot, the roots resist. I resist. *I'm* still in her soil – to some degree. We're captives of the past. The ghost of her clings, as they say in the song.

CYNTHIA. Yes, if you let it.

RICHARD. We can't help it. Good grief, do you understand nothing?

CYNTHIA. You've got to *shake* it off. And that you're unwilling to do, all of you.

Pause.

RICHARD. All right. I'll do anything that makes you happy. What do you want?

CYNTHIA. I want your support. I'm only asking for your support.

RICHARD. To do what?

CYNTHIA. No fairy-stories for a start.

RICHARD. You mean wean them off?

CYNTHIA. Just don't tell them any.

RICHARD. What if they ask? My heart would break.

CYNTHIA. Let it. Now I'd like a drink.

RICHARD. Scotch?

CYNTHIA. Yes.

He pours a drink.

RICHARD. Let me give you one piece of advice. I love you and I'll help you in any way I can. But don't try to fight her. She's got too many allies.

Fade out.

Fade in the house.

CYNTHIA. I could take them away for the Easter holidays. We could go to the cottage in Yorkshire – your gingerbread house. I could finish my book. It is peaceful up there, isn't it?

RICHARD. Oh, yes, it's peaceful all right.

CYNTHIA. You sound doubtful.

RICHARD. How long were you thinking of?

CYNTHIA. Only the week. You could drive up on Friday night.

RICHARD. It's just that they spent so many holidays there with Mary. The happiest times they've had, I imagine.

CYNTHIA (*sympathetic*). And you think I'll spoil those memories?

RICHARD. No, it's got to be done, I can see that. The house needs an airing. Yes, go ahead. Only be careful.

CYNTHIA. Careful?

RICHARD. It's a rather dangerous part of the world. I mean the moor. It's riddled with old lead mines. Shafts that were never sealed off and got overgrown. I was always terrified they'd fall down one of them. Mary had a nasty moment once. The ground suddenly opened beneath her. She just had time to spring to one side. You'll have to keep a sharp eye on them.

CYNTHIA. What's the house like?

RICHARD. Comfortable, shabby, four bedrooms, an attic. The most enormous ancient kitchen range with an oven you could squeeze a whole cow into. It stands all by itself on the edge of the moor. Not another house in sight.

CYNTHIA. Why do you call it gingerbread?

RICHARD. Well, that was Mary's name for it. It's a fine sturdy stone building, basically Georgian and plain, only at some point in its history some whimsical fellow came along and decorated the front with weird patterns in brown plaster. Owls and frogs and rabbits and other little creatures.

CYNTHIA. Awful.

RICHARD. I think it's rather a lark. Yes, and the skylarks should be singing over the moor – curlews – peewits – daffodils coming out. I really do envy you.

Fade out.

Fade in the moor.
A curlew is calling. KATE *and* HARRY *are shouting and laughing in the distance.*

Fade out.

Fade in the kitchen.
CYNTHIA *is whisking an egg.*
The door opens.

CYNTHIA. Hello, darling, did you wipe your feet, dinner won't be long, where's Harry?

KATE. Yes, I did. He went upstairs. He's tired out. We've been making a heffalump trap.

CYNTHIA. Oh, yes? On the moor?

KATE. Yes, we got a pile of bracken and a fence post.

CYNTHIA. Is that out of *Winnie the Pooh*? A heffalump trap?

KATE. Yes, of course.

CYNTHIA. Then I don't want to hear about it. Go and wash your hands. Your father will be here soon.

A telephone is ringing.

CYNTHIA. All right, Kate, I'll get it.

The phone is answered.

CYNTHIA. Gimmerbeck 2438.

RICHARD. Cynthia?

CYNTHIA. Richard!

KATE (*off*). Daddy!

RICHARD. I'm speaking from Warrington. I had to get off the motorway. There was a massive tailback. Some kind of pile-up ahead. So I'll make my way across country. Could be about an hour late.

CYNTHIA. Poor pet. What a nuisance. So we'll expect you about eight?

RICHARD. Sorry if it puts you out.

CYNTHIA. No, I'll just lower the oven, that's all.

RICHARD. How are the children?

CYNTHIA. They're grand. You'll notice a big change in Harry. He's grown quite plump.

RICHARD. Grown plump in one week?

CYNTHIA. Yes, I'm fattening him up. I only wish Kate would eat more.

The door opens and closes.

CYNTHIA. Would you like a word with her?

RICHARD. Yes please.

CYNTHIA. Oh, she's gone. She was here a second ago.

RICHARD. Is Harry there?

CYNTHIA. No, he's upstairs somewhere. All right, you'll want to push on. I'll expect you at eight. Missing you.

RICHARD. Take care of my babies, won't you?

CYNTHIA. Of course. Goodbye Richard. Drive carefully.

Fade out.

KATE *going up bare creaking stairs.*

KATE. Harry? (*More stairs.*) Harry? Are you up there? (*More stairs.*) Harry, where are you?

She opens a creaking door.

Harry, are you in here? (*Pause.*) Where can he be?

A door closes.

Harry, are you up there?

She climbs more stairs, then stops.

Harry? Harry? You're here somewhere.

A door opens suddenly. HARRY *makes a frightening muffled noise.* KATE *screams.*

HARRY. Hush, hush! It's all right. It's only me. Look.

KATE (*sobbing and laughing*). Oh, Harry, Harry!

HARRY. Hush. Come on, in here.

The door closes.

KATE. Don't put that thing on your head again.

HARRY. It's only a gas mask.

KATE. Well it's horrible.

HARRY. They had them in the war.

KATE. What for?

HARRY. To frighten the Germans.

Pause.

KATE. Harry, we've got to run away.

HARRY. Run away? It's nearly supper-time.

KATE. Cynthia said . . . Cynthia said . . . .

HARRY. Cynthia said what?

KATE. She's going to eat you.

HARRY (*laughing*). She's what? Oh, rhubarb.

KATE. She's going to cook you – in the oven.

HARRY. You're trying to scare me. I'll put this mask on again.

KATE. Honestly, honestly, she was just speaking to Daddy on the phone. She said she was fattening you up.

HARRY. Fattening me up?

KATE. Fattening you up.

HARRY. What do you mean?

KATE. She said you'd grown quite plump.

HARRY. No, I haven't.

KATE. Yes you have.

HARRY. Well . . . that doesn't mean anything.

KATE. It does. It means she's going to put you in the oven.

HARRY. No it doesn't. Not necessarily.

KATE. Yes! This is her last chance before Daddy gets here. That's why she's been fattening you up.

CYNTHIA (*calling from below*). Children! Harry! Kate! Are you up there?

KATE. Shh! Don't answer.

Pause.

CYNTHIA (*from below*). Children? Are you up there?

HARRY (*calling*). Yes, Cynthia!

KATE. Oh, what have you done?

HARRY (*calling*). Coming, Cynthia!

KATE. Harry, no!

He opens the door.

HARRY. Oh, don't be silly. Come on.

Fade out.

Fade in the kitchen. CYNTHIA *is laying the table.*

CYNTHIA. Come on, you can give me a hand laying the table. Katie, get the glasses out of the sideboard.

KATE. The wine glasses?

CYNTHIA. Yes, please, the big ones. And Harry, just open the oven door a couple of inches. It's much too hot in there.

KATE. Harry!

CYNTHIA. I beg your pardon, Kate?

HARRY. Daddy doesn't let us near the oven – when it's hot.

CYNTHIA. Well, I'm letting you. You're a big boy now. You're
perfectly capable of opening an oven door, aren't you? Aren't you?

HARRY. Well . . .

KATE. No, Harry!

CYNTHIA. What nonsense. (*She moves to the oven.*) Come here, Harry,
let me show you, it's perfectly safe if you use the oven gloves.
(*Pause.*) Come on. What are you frightened of?

HARRY. Nothing.

CYNTHIA. Then come to me.

HARRY. I'd rather wait – till Daddy comes.

CYNTHIA. Oh, very well.

> *She opens the oven door.*

There, it's open. No harm came to me, did it? Do you want to
look inside at the joint cooking?

HARRY. No thank you.

CYNTHIA. Very well. (*Pause.*) Harry, hand me the carving knife.

HARRY. Why do you want the carving knife?

CYNTHIA. I want to sharpen it.

KATE. Harry!

HARRY. Oh, shut up.

> *He rummages in the knife drawer and gives her the knife.*

CYNTHIA. Thank you, Harry. What a strange mood you're in
tonight.

> *She starts sharpening the carving knife.*

Put out the dinner plates, will you? Katie, we still want those
wine glasses.

> *A moment or two of the sound of plates and glasses and of the knife being
> sharpened.*

CYNTHIA. Draw the curtains, will you, Kate?

KATE. All right. (*Gasps*). Oh, no! Look through the window!

CYNTHIA. What's the matter?

KATE. No, don't look!

CYNTHIA. What is it? What have you seen?

KATE. The new moon. I've seen the new moon through glass. That's bad luck.

CYNTHIA. Good God, is that all? You little fool, I nearly cut myself.

KATE. But it's bad luck. Somebody will die. Mummy said.

CYNTHIA. Rubbish.

KATE. You looked! You both looked through the window. Quickly – we've all got to turn round three times. There – I'm safe. Harry, quickly, turn round.

CYNTHIA. Harry, you'll do no such thing. It's all nonsense.

KATE. Harry, you must, you'll die!

CYNTHIA. Harry, I absolutely forbid – Harry!

KATE. Good, it's all right, we're both safe now.

CYNTHIA. I've never heard such wicked, superstitious claptrap.

KATE. Turn round, Cynthia. Please!

CYNTHIA. Me?

KATE. You'll die! You'll die!

CYNTHIA. Katie, don't be so stupid. I never met a more idiotic, senseless child. You really do make me sick with all your nonsense.

HARRY. Shut up!

CYNTHIA. Are you talking to me? What did you say?

HARRY. Shut up! Don't talk to my sister like that. My mummy hit you in the mouth and I'm glad!

CYNTHIA. For God's sake stop resurrecting your mother! Will you get it into your heads once and for all? Your mother is dead. Underground, in a box, she's been there more than a year, she's rotting, rotting.

HARRY. }
KATE. } No!

CYNTHIA. Yes, rotting!

HARRY. }
KATE. } No!

CYNTHIA. Eaten by worms!

KATE *screams.*

The CHILDREN *burst through the door and upstairs.*

Come back! Where do you think you're going? Children!

She knocks a glass off the table and it shatters.

Oh, damn! Children, children! You'll come back down those stairs if I have to drag you.

Crossfade to upstairs.

KATE. She's got the carving knife. That's why she was sharpening it.

HARRY. Hush. She'll get tired. She'll go away.

KATE. No, listen, she's coming. Come on, up, up.

HARRY. Not up there. That leads to the attic. We'll be trapped.

KATE. Which way then?

HARRY. Along this corridor.

Ghostly music behind.

KATE. Corridor? I don't remember this corridor.

HARRY. Quick! She's coming. (*They scamper away.*)

CYNTHIA (*approaching*). Children, please come down. I'm sorry if I upset you. Daddy will soon be here. Let's all be friends.

HARRY (*grim whisper*). No!

CYNTHIA. Children, do you hear? Come down at once! Don't be so foolish. (*Pause.*) All right, I'm going to switch all the lights off.

Six light switches click off.

Now if you don't come down I'll come up and look for *you* – in the dark.

Pause.

KATE (*whisper*). Harry!

HARRY. Shh!

KATE. We'd better go down.

HARRY. No, we'll go up.

KATE. There isn't any more up.

HARRY. Yes there is. I saw another staircase just before the light went off. Come on.

KATE. I can't see.

HARRY. Hold my hand. Right. This way. Careful now.

They climb away. We rejoin them at the top.

KATE. Where are we?

HARRY. I don't know.

KATE. We've gone up four flights. I only ever remember three – counting the attic.

HARRY. We've gone higher than the attic.

KATE. How could we?

HARRY. I don't know.

KATE. Listen, she's coming.

HARRY. I can feel a draught. There must be another staircase. Yes. Over here. Come on. Hurry.

They climb away and we rejoin them at the top.

KATE. Harry, where are we now?

HARRY. We must be near the top.

KATE. We must be *past* the top. Harry, I thought this house only had four bedrooms. (*Pause.*) Harry! Where are you?

HARRY. It's all right. I'm here.

KATE. What are you doing?

HARRY. Feeling for another door.

KATE. We can't go any higher.

HARRY. Quick. I've found it.

He lifts an iron latch and opens a door. Echo effect and wind.

HARRY. Yes, another staircase. Give me your hand.

KATE. Where are you?

HARRY. Here. Now come on. (*They climb.*) Careful, the stairs are made of stone. They twist round and round . . . like a corkscrew.

KATE. I'm cold. Why is it so windy?

HARRY. Look up there. Chinks in the wall. You can see the sky.

KATE. It's a tower. Harry, this house doesn't *have* a tower.

They climb away and we rejoin them at the top.

What's the matter? Why have you stopped?

HARRY. This door. It won't open.

KATE. Well push.

HARRY. There's a big rusty iron ring. It's stuck. If only I could turn it.

KATE. Harry, she's still coming!

HARRY. I can't turn it!

KATE. She's coming, she's coming!

HARRY. If only I – there – there – it's moving – it's moving – there!

A big door crashes open.

Come on, quick, inside! Close it!

Door crashes shut. Lose wind and echo.

CYNTHIA (*calmly*). Hello, children. Got you.

KATE *screams.*

Scream to your heart's content, little one. But nobody will hear you. Not up here.

HARRY. What room . . . what room . . . ?

CYNTHIA. Yes, Harry?

HARRY. What room is this?

CYNTHIA. My very private parlour. I've been waiting for you very patiently.

HARRY. Quick, Kate! (*Running away.*) Through that door!

KATE *runs away screaming.*

CYNTHIA. Stop! Kate! Harry! Come back! (*Laughing.*) There's no getting away!

HARRY (*running*). Find the back stairs! Find the back stairs!

KATE (*running*). What back stairs? There are no back stairs!

CYNTHIA *is heard laughing in the distance.*

She's coming! She's coming!

HARRY. Run! Just run!

They run along a seemingly endless echoing corridor, stopping to open four doors. The final door is banged shut.

Both CHILDREN *stand breathless.*

There they are! The back stairs. Come on – down!

KATE. Why are they so steep?

HARRY. Never mind that. Down, down, down!

KATE. No! I can't go any further. I can't. I can't.

HARRY. Down, down, down. (*He starts running down.*)

KATE. Wait for me! I'm coming! (*She starts running down.*) Harry! Not so fast! You're flying! You're flying!

CYNTHIA's *laughter is heard behind.*

HARRY. Come on! Come on! She's coming!

KATE. You're flying! You're flying!

HARRY. She's coming!

KATE. I'm falling!

HARRY. She's coming!

KATE. Falling! Falling!

CYNTHIA (*distant*). I'm coming, coming!

KATE. I'm flying.

CYNTHIA. Coming.

KATE. Flying, flying.

Sudden silence.

A doorknob being rattled.

HARRY. Stop! Stop. A door.

KATE. Well open it.

HARRY. The knob's loose. It just goes round and round in my hand. Wait. There's a key.

A key rattled in a keyhole.

The door opens.

There. Come inside. Quick. Close it.

The door closes.

KATE. The kitchen!

HARRY. Yes.

KATE. We're back in the kitchen. The table laid. Look, a broken glass. Oh, no, that was Mummy's.

HARRY. Never mind. Out. Come on.

The door opens onto the windy moor.

KATE. Where are we going?

HARRY. The moor.

KATE. I'll gather up this glass so Daddy won't see.

HARRY. No, there's no time.

KATE. I won't be a minute.

The glass is gathered up.

An inner door opens.

CYNTHIA (*fondly*). So there you are. I've looked everywhere. Careful you don't cut yourself, Kate.

HARRY. Kate! Come on!

She drops the pieces of glass.

CYNTHIA. Stop! Where are you going now? The dinner – Oh, come back!

On the moor.

Children! Children! You haven't got your coats! (*To herself.*) I've a good mind to leave them out, the little sillies. (*Calling.*) Kate!

Harry! (*Fading.*) Children!

KATE (*fade in*). Harry! Slow down. I can't keep up.

HARRY. All right, have a breather.

KATE. Do you know where we're going?

HARRY. Of course I do. Not far now.

KATE. Whereabouts is it? Do you remember?

HARRY. You see the thorn tree – against the sky?

KATE. Where? Yes, I see it.

HARRY. Well, it's between that and the big pointed rock.
Now come on.

KATE. Look at the moon. She didn't turn round.

HARRY. Well that's her lookout. Quiet. Is she still coming?

KATE. I don't know.

HARRY. Quiet.

CYNTHIA (*distant*). Children! Children!

KATE. She's right over there. How did she get over there. She'll
never find us.

HARRY. Better give her a shout. Over here!

KATE. Over here!

HARRY. Cynthia!

KATE (*fading*). We're here, Cynthia!

CYNTHIA (*fading in – close to tears*). Oh, drat them, damn them, curse
them, blast them. Mustn't lose sight of the house – no – blazing
lights – keep it in sight. Children! You'll get hopelessly lost!
You'll have us *all* hopelessly lost!

KATE (*distant*). Cynthia!

HARRY. Over here, Cynthia!

CYNTHIA. They're leading me on, that's what, they're deliberately
leading me on. (*She yells:*) I shall go back and tell your father!
(*Pause.*) Good Lord, the house, where am I? I've lost the house.

Pause.

HARRY (*quite close*). Cynthia.

KATE. Cynthia.

HARRY. This way, Cynthia.

CYNTHIA (*uncertainly*). Children? What are you up to? Be sensible
now. You're behind that rock, aren't you? (*Steely.*) Right! I know
exactly where you are and I can run faster than you. (*Moving.*) Yes,

I can certainly run faster than the little – oh! – my feet! ground sinking! – help! aaahhh! (*She falls down the shaft.*)

Echo atmosphere.

(*Feebly.*) Help. Help. Help me. Please help me.

KATE (*at the top*). Cynthia.

CYNTHIA. Help! I'm on a ledge! It's crumbling! Get help!

KATE. Cynthia.

CYNTHIA. Don't you hear? The ledge is breaking. Bring help. Tell them a rope.

KATE. It's your own fault. You should have turned round for the moon. Goodnight, Cynthia.

CYNTHIA. No! Don't go!

HARRY. Goodnight, Cynthia.

CYNTHIA. Don't go! Don't leave me!

A few rocks slip and tumble.

Oh, my God, no please, this isn't happening to me, this isn't HAPPENING! (*She screams as the ledge collapses.*)

A big rockfall.

Fade out.

Fade in the kitchen.
Outside in the hall the CHILDREN *are excitedly greeting* RICHARD – *laughter and shouts of 'Daddy' and general hopping up and down.*

The door opens into the kitchen.

RICHARD (*sniffs*). Hmm, smells good.

HARRY. Leg of lamb, yum yum.

KATE. What did you bring us? What did you bring us?

RICHARD. Never you mind. No – careful with that. It's a bottle of wine. Where's Cynthia?

KATE. She went out for a walk.

RICHARD. In the dark?

HARRY. For some fresh air.

RICHARD. Well – listen here – does that mean we've got time for a quick fairy-story – before she gets back?

KATE. Yes, yes!

RICHARD. Now what shall it be? *Hansel and Gretel?*

Fade out.

MYTHS AND LEGACIES

by Valerie Windsor

To Kay Patrick

Valerie Windsor was born in Essex but has spent most of her life in the north of England. She trained at the Rose Bruford College of Speech and Drama and worked both as an actress and as a teacher (as well as doing several other odd and generally unsuccessful jobs) before starting to write. She has written a number of radio plays and dramatised features including *Variation on the Snow Queen* which won a Pye/Society of Authors' award. Television work includes episodes of the Mersey Television series *Brookside*. Her first stage play was produced in 1987, and she has recently completed a novel. She is married with two children and a cat.

Myths and Legacies was first broadcast on BBC Radio 4 on
3 March 1986. The cast was as follows:

SISTER JULIAN/JULIA	Rosalie Crutchley
JULIA *as a child*	Claire Webzell
EDWARD	Patrick Stewart
EDWARD *as a child*	Philip Glancy
WILLIAM	Daniel Massey
WILLIAM *as a child*	Tamlyn Robins
TREVOR	John Basham
DORA/WOMAN/NUN	Jane Leonard
FATHER	Peter Laird
OFFICER/LAWYER/WAITER	Christopher Kent
MEDICAL OFFICER/McLEOD/2nd LAWYER	Nigel Caliburn

Director: Kay Patrick
Running time, as broadcast: 88 minutes, 56 seconds.

A convent. SISTER JULIAN *and* TREVOR *approach along a stone-flagged passage.*

SISTER JULIAN (*approaching*). Through a grille in the wall. Yes, it's true. But recently . . . .

She pushes open the door to the parlour and they enter.

This is the parlour, we receive our guests here nowadays. I do hope you'll be able to find a comfortable chair.

TREVOR (*sitting*). Thank you.

SISTER JULIAN. To tell you the truth, Mr Norman, we were expecting you rather earlier than this.

TREVOR. Yes, I'm sorry. I . . . .

SISTER JULIAN. You look very uncomfortable there.

TREVOR. I think the springs are broken.

SISTER JULIAN. Try that one.

TREVOR *moves.*

TREVOR (*clears his throat*). So . . . you got my letter?

SISTER JULIAN. I don't receive letters, Mr Norman. This is an enclosed order. A silent order. We work in the garden and we think. Or pray, if you prefer to call it praying. Finally, you see, a Voltairean solution. I understand from Reverend Mother that you're writing a book?

TREVOR. Yes, I . . . .

SISTER JULIAN. A book about us?

TREVOR. Well . . . actually . . . Well, specifically, of course, the idea is . . . . What I want to do is to write a book about Edward Tillotson. I believe he was your cousin?

SISTER JULIAN. About Edward?

TREVOR. He was a remarkable man.

SISTER JULIAN (*weakly*). Yes.

TREVOR. Extraordinary.

SISTER JULIAN. Yes, I suppose one could say that.

TREVOR. The most powerfully inspirational character . . . .

SISTER JULIAN (*winded by the idea*). Powerfully inspirational?

TREVOR. I think history will see him as one of the great men of this century . . . .

SISTER JULIAN. Tell me . . . in what precise capacity do you find him so . . . ?

TREVOR. Well, for a start . . .

SISTER JULIAN. . . . what did you say? Powerfully inspirational?

TREVOR. . . . for a start, those incredible expeditions across South Yemen and up to the Gulf . . .

SISTER JULIAN. Yes, I see . . . .

TREVOR. . . . and then from virtually nothing . . . to build from nothing the entire Tillotson McCleod empire . . . .

SISTER JULIAN. Yes. (*Pause.*) So you're doing research for a book about Edward Tillotson. Is that right?

TREVOR. Yes.

SISTER JULIAN. And you come to speak to me?

TREVOR. Well, I believe you're the only surviving relative. Actually, it was very difficult finding you. I thought . . . .

SISTER JULIAN (*suddenly and firmly*). No. No, I'm afraid it won't do. A book about Edward? I can't allow it. If you intend to write about my cousin Edward, then you must also write about my cousin William. They were twins. You can't write about the one without the other.

TREVOR. No, well, of course, I had hoped you'd be able to . . . . But the thing is . . . I mean William wasn't really . . . from what I understand at any rate, he wasn't . . . I will mention him, of course, but . . . (*Back to* EDWARD.) I mean, if you're looking for someone, some figure, who might exemplify what's . . . you know . . . what's particularly admirable in a man . . . I mean everything: courage, endurance, single-mindedness, vision, the power to make things happen . . . . That kind of entrepreneurial skill that no one seems to have any more. I admire him enormously.

SISTER JULIAN. I see you do. Yes.

TREVOR. He went out and he made what he wanted out of his life. He wasn't in any way limited by other people's ideas . . . .

SISTER JULIAN. Or feelings . . . .

TREVOR. A few more people like him in the world, and perhaps we wouldn't . . . .

SISTER JULIAN. Well, as you see, I've retired from the world. I can hardly offer an opinion. Nevertheless, I think one should always be on one's guard. One should be very careful in one's assessment of what the world needs.
Tell me, Mr Norman, what kind of things do you write? Have you written biography before?

TREVOR. I've written a book about the European car industry. That's coming out in May.

SISTER JULIAN. So you're not a novelist?

TREVOR. A novelist? No, I'm a journalist. Well, by trade I am, but I hope that . . . .

SISTER JULIAN. I would have preferred a novelist, but never mind. There we are. Is that chair more comfortable, Mr Norman?

TREVOR (*bewildered*). Um . . . yes. Yes it's fine.

SISTER JULIAN (*having made a decision*). Good. Because I intend to tell you a story. I think it may help you.
Once upon a time . . . That's the proper way to start a story, isn't it? Certain kinds of story, anyway. We were brought up on them, my cousins and I. Once upon a time . . . well, to be more precise, 1896 or thereabouts, a little girl called Dora . . .

TREVOR (*at last something makes sense*). Ah yes. Dora. (*He leans over to get papers out of his briefcase.*) Do you mean Dora Barnes? Now . . . (*Sorting out papers.*) she was . . . Is it all right if I take notes?

SISTER JULIAN. She was our nursery maid, I mention her because she was there when Edward was born. The very beginning . . . .

DORA (*a voice coming out of the past*). I'm not going to tell you if you're going to fidget.
Well, sit still like a good girl and then maybe I will.
She used to say to me: 'Dora, come and sit in my room and read to me.' I was straight out of school, see, so I could read very nicely. With all the proper expression. She had . . . what is it? That illness. What's the proper word? She was very thin. Couldn't bear the light. She couldn't bear *him*, your uncle, stamping through the house with his dogs yapping round him. 'Come and sit in my room and read to me,' she said. Her stomach swelled and swelled until it took up all the bed, but the rest of her shrivelled away. 'Oh, Dora,' she said, 'this thing inside me is eating me up.' Consumption! That's the word. That's it. That's what she had.

'It's a monster,' she said, 'a two headed monster. Crunch. Munch. Listen to it in there. Dora,' she said, 'don't go. Don't leave me.' They wanted me out of the room. They said I was too young. But she held on to my wrist so tight they couldn't prise open her fingers. (*A sudden indignant thought.*) And another thing! They weren't born like Mr Tillotson said at all. Your uncle says . . .

FATHER'S VOICE (*telling a story to the boys*). And the first came out red like an hairy garment. And after that came his brother out . . . .

DORA. He's got it all muddled. It wasn't like that at all.

FATHER'S VOICE. Two nations. Two manner of people . . .

DORA. There was a good half hour between them. He says William was hanging onto Edward's heel but he wasn't.
'Well, Dora,' she said, 'is it a monster? Is it? How many heads has it got? And she tried to laugh. But it turned into a cough. And then she couldn't stop. The blood shot out of her mouth and streamed between her fingers and nothing would stop it. She was dead nearly ten minutes before William was delivered.

FATHER'S VOICE. And the one people shall be stronger than the other people and the elder shall serve the younger . . . .

DORA. Don't you take any notice what he says. That's all nonsense. He's got it all muddled up with one of them Bible stories. Or *Tales of Troy.* Something like that. King Arthur. I never liked those stories much. Used to give William nightmares when he was little. And Nanny Curtis . . . or Nanny Bosworth . . . I don't know, there were so many of them . . . they used to say: 'I'm sorry, Mr Tillotson, but I'm going to have to put my foot down about this. I really don't think that story's suitable for little minds.'

FATHER'S VOICE. Indeed not, madam. You therefore have my permission to leave the room. Do you hear me?

DORA. He made their lives a misery. In and out. Questioning. Finding fault.
'My sons will eat red meat,' he said. 'They must learn not to cry when they fall down . . . .'

FATHER (*now as if in the room*). They will learn not to be afraid of dogs, or the sound of a shot-gun. What's this nonsense you've got on the wall? A for Apple, B for Bird!
Madam, we can do better than that. A for Arthur. B for Bellerophon. C for Charlemagne . . . .

DORA (*subversive whisper, to comfort them*). A for Alice, B for Beauty and the Beast. C for Cinderella . . . .

FATHER. What? What's that?

DORA (*to* FATHER). It's only fairy-tales, sir.

FATHER. And you're to take no notice of their nightmares.

If William has another nightmare you will not take him into your bed. They will eat their crusts and take cold baths every morning. I will not allow candles in their bedroom. A man must learn to outface darkness. What else is civilisation if not that?

DORA. 'Madam,' he said, 'I find in this nursery no concept of God or Honour . . . .'

FATHER. A pagan place full of apples and birds. Take that nonsense off the wall!

DORA. So naturally none of them would stay longer than a month. Nanny Bosworth. Nanny Curtis. I've forgotten half their names. And then the last one packed her bag and was driven to the station and nobody turned up to take her place.

FATHER. Do you hear me! Never. Never again. Not one more. You can run a nursery, can't you, Dora?

DORA. Yes, sir. I think so, sir.

FATHER. Good. Well then. You get on with it.

DORA. Yes, sir.

FATHER (*shouting from slight distance*). Durrant! Where are you? Where are my boots? Get those bloody dogs out of the way. R for Roland, S for Saladin, T for Theseus. Write that down for them. I won't have you interfering, Dora.
William still having nightmares, is he?

DORA. Sometimes, sir.

FATHER. Be a damn good thing when that boy goes off to prep school. (*Going.*)

DORA. Yes, sir.

The door shuts behind FATHER.

(*Softly, very close, out of silence:*) It's all right. Nothing will hurt you. Listen, I'll tell you the story about the princess and the frog . . . .

FATHER (*stamping along the corridor*). Dora!

DORA. Yes, sir?

FATHER (*coming in*). What are you up to now? Where are you? Now look here . . . look at this . . . you'll have to deal with this, Dora. You'll have to fetch her from the station. I don't know what you say to a little girl.

DORA. What little girl?

FATHER. Read it. Read it. It's all there in the letter. My brother's little girl. I'll leave it all to you, Dora. You sort it out. (*Going.*)

DORA (*as the door closes, softly*). Are you ready? Once upon a time there was a princess with long golden hair who liked to play in the palace garden . . . .

The parlour

TREVOR. Um . . . this little girl . . . ?

SISTER JULIAN. Yes, that was me. My father was in the Indian Civil
Service. But for health reasons he decided to leave me in my
uncle's care rather than risk exposing me to the Indian climate.
Probably a sensible decision. It killed both my parents within
five years.
   I must have been about three or four when this happened . . .
when I was sent to live with my uncle. I don't remember it.
My first clear memory was of this voice thundering up and down
the passages . . . .

FATHER (*distant voice thundering and echoing*). Dora!

DORA. Yes, sir?

FATHER (*approaching*). Where's my niece? Where is she?
(*Coming into the nursery.*) Put her coat on. Find some boots. I want
to try her on horseback this afternoon. See what sort of a seat
she's got on a horse.

DORA. Yes, sir.

FATHER. Well, miss. And how's your school-work going? Can she
read yet? Are you teaching her to read, Dora?

DORA. Yes, sir. She's learning her alphabet very nicely.

FATHER. Don't know why she won't look at me when I speak to
her. Is she a deceitful child? Come on, pipe up, girl. Here's
another question for you. Let's see if you know this. Now then.
(*Thinking.*) What about this? How did Perseus outwit Medusa?

DORA. No, sir. She can't answer that. She doesn't know any of
those stories yet.

FATHER. Doesn't know any!

DORA. No, sir.

FATHER. Why doesn't she know any? Good God, woman, those are
the stories we breathe in with our first cry. We've always known
them. What rubbish are you filling her head with, Dora? I know
your airy fairy rubbish. You mind what you're up to. Well, miss.
Better take you in hand, eh? (*Going.*) Let's see how you sit a horse.
Do you know any of your Bible stories?

The door closes.
Fade to silence.

The parlour.

SISTER JULIAN. That's what I remember. Sitting on a horse and
sliding off. Questions being fired at me. The sense that I was a
disappointment. I'm afraid I hardly remember my cousins at that

time at all. They were sent away to prep school and after that . . .
after they went . . . my uncle seldom went near the nursery. He
wasn't interested in me. For years Dora and I were left pretty
much to our own devices. I spent most of my time playing in the
garden . . . .

The garden. Distantly some BOYS *aged about 14 are playing cricket. Close to,*
JULIA, *aged about 10, is playing by the pond and perhaps humming tunelessly
to establish her presence there.*

BOYS (*after the thwacking noise of ball against bat*).
 – Oh, well played.
 – Played!
 – Go on, Haraldson. Run!

WILLIAM. Christ, where's it going? Catch it, Edward.

EDWARD (*approaching at a run*). It's going to land in the pond!

WILLIAM. Catch it! Catch him out!

A loud splash as the ball lands in the pond.

EDWARD. Damn it! (*He sees* JULIA.) Oh, I say, I'm sorry. Did I
 frighten you? What on earth are you doing?
  You can speak, you know. It's all right. I'm not suddenly going
 to turn into a frog. No, wait a minute, that's the wrong way
 round, isn't it? (*He pulls off his shoes.*) Keep an eye on my shoes,
 will you? I'm going to have to wade in. (*Wading into the water.*)
 Suppose I did turn into a frog. What would you do? You'd have
 to take me indoors in your pocket and let me eat from your
 golden plate . . . .

BOYS. – Hurry up.
  – Come on, Tillotson.

EDWARD. Do you know what I think that story means? I think it
 means that girls who are particularly fond of gold should never
 turn their noses up at fat warty little men with slimy manners
 because they're bound to turn out to be millionaires.

WILLIAM (*calling*). Edward, stop mucking about!

EDWARD (*finding the ball*). Got it.
  You're always playing round here, aren't you? Or in the bushes or
 somewhere. I watch you sometimes. (*Over his shoulder as he goes.*)
 You want to be careful near the pond. It's quite deep in the
 middle. (*To the* BOYS:) Hoy! Catch!

BOY. Who's that you were talking to?

EDWARD (*on his way back to the game*). No one. Just a cousin of ours.

The parlour.

SISTER JULIAN. I was very shocked by that.

TREVOR. By . . . ?

SISTER JULIAN. By what he said. That wasn't what the story meant.
It didn't mean anything. It simply was. I still played in the garden
but the pleasure of it was never as powerful as it had been.
I started looking for meanings. I asked Dora about it. I said, 'What
does that story *mean*?' 'Well, I don't know,' she said, 'I expect
what it means is that you've got to be a nice kind little girl and
look after poor little creatures who aren't as fortunate as you are.'
    Or to put it another way, I suppose, 'Inasmuch as ye have done
it unto one of the least of these my brethren, ye have done it
unto me.'
    I said: 'I don't think it means that at all.'
    'Well,' she said, 'it all depends how you interpret it, doesn't it?
It could mean all sorts of things.'
It's a very powerful story, that one. Don't you think so?

A bell starts to ring.

TREVOR (*all his uneasiness suddenly returned*). What does that mean?

SISTER JULIAN. It's the bell for the office.

TREVOR (*uneasy*). Oh, I see. Well, look, had I . . . ?

SISTER JULIAN. Sit down, Mr Norman.

TREVOR. I don't want to . . . (cause any trouble).

JULIA. I said sit down.
    (*He sits.*)
    Thank you.
    I've decided not to say the office tonight. I haven't the time.
    Don't argue with me. Lord knows whether I shall have the
    opportunity to speak out again. One has to take whatever chance
    is offered. Perhaps I should have spoken out before. You come
    here saying you want to write a book about Edward. You come
    here full of his praises. You think the world would be a better
    place if there were more men like Edward in it. Is that a generally
    held opinion nowadays? Then you must write this story down.
    You must remind people. I've been silent too long. It's too easy
    to cultivate one's garden and say nothing. (*He tries to interrupt.*)
    No, sit down. Listen. You must take notes. This is what I want
    you to write. Once upon a time there were two young men.
    Twins. Barely out of public school . . . .

A recruiting office.

OFFICER. Name?

EDWARD (*very military*). Tillotson, sir, Double L.

OFFICER (*looking up*). Good God. Haven't I just seen you?

EDWARD. My younger brother, sir. William Tillotson. I'm
Edward Tillotson.

OFFICER. Twins?

EDWARD. Yes, sir.

OFFICER. Good Lord. Peas in a pod. Must be damned annoying for you.

EDWARD. Yes, sir.

OFFICER (*sorting out papers*). Yes, I see. Tillotson E.J.

Realises that he has bad news to impart.

Ah. Yes. At ease, Tillotson.

EDWARD. Sir.

OFFICER. Well now, look here, I've got the MO's report, Tillotson, and the fact is . . . damned bad luck under the circumstances. 'Now all the youth of England are on fire,' and all that. 'Honour's thought', etc. Still, there we are. Can't be helped. Nothing too serious, I'm glad to say. Small spot on the apex of the right lung.

EDWARD. What do you mean 'small spot'?

OFFICER (*awkwardly*). Well, I gather from the MO's report there's a family history of it . . . .

EDWARD (*who's completely forgotten military protocol*). History of what?

OFFICER. Lung trouble, Tillotson.

EDWARD. Where is this report? I don't believe it. You mean tuberculosis?

OFFICER. 'Fraid so.

EDWARD (*after a pause*). Both of us?

OFFICER. Apparently not. Tillotson W.G. A1.

EDWARD. I don't believe you. It's a mistake. There's nothing wrong with my lungs. It's some stupid mistake. I want another examination. I want a second opinion.

OFFICER. Look, why don't you sit down for a minute . . . .

EDWARD. You can't take William and not me. William and I, we . . . you can't. I *must* go. We decided. Both of us. Together. William and I. This is a mistake. I want to see the MO again.

The MO's office.

MO. Any weight loss?

EDWARD. No.

MO. Night sweats?

EDWARD. No.

MO. Do you suffer from headaches?

EDWARD. Never.

MO. Say 'ninety-nine'.

EDWARD. Ninety-nine.

MO (*listening through a stethoscope*). And again.

EDWARD. Ninety-nine.

MO. Yes, you see, there it is. Listen. Can you hear that? Do you cough a lot in the morning?

EDWARD. I don't think so. No.

MO. Well, I tell you what . . . things could be a lot worse. Looks to me like we've caught this in good time. Pretty good chance it'll clear up completely. Six months in the mountains somewhere. Maybe a year.

EDWARD. Look, sir, if it's not that bad . . . I mean, I don't feel ill. Couldn't you . . . ?

MO. Sorry, Tillotson. Out of the question.

The house. Breakfast. The FATHER *is now a very old man, almost blind.*

FATHER. For what we are about to receive . . . sit down. Sit down. What's all this?

DORA. It's the post, sir.

FATHER. Well, good God, don't give it to me. Can't see a damned thing these days. Give it to someone else.

DORA. Careful with your spoon, sir.

FATHER. I can manage. Stop fussing.

DORA. Hold the egg cup.

FATHER. Stop fussing me, Dora. Dim-witted women fussing me.

DORA. I'll get a cloth. (*She gets up and goes.*)

EDWARD (*nastily*). Letter for you, William. Official.

FATHER. What is it? Speak up.

WILLIAM (*awkward*). My commission's come through.

FATHER. Where? Where is it? Show me. Read it to me. Why are you mumbling? Do you think to spare Edward's feelings? None of your business. Come on. I want to hear.

WILLIAM. George, by the grace of God . . . .

FATHER. Speak up.

WILLIAM. All of it?

FATHER. All of it. Listen to this, Julia. What do you think of this, eh? Your cousin.

EDWARD. Excuse me.

FATHER. Sit down.

WILLIAM (*continued reluctance*) . . . grace of God . . . um . . . (*Cutting.*)
We, reposing especial trust and confidence in your loyalty,
courage and good conduct . . .

FATHER. Hah! You hear that? Go on.

WILLIAM. . . . do by these presents constitute and appoint you to be
an officer in our land forces . . . .

FATHER (*leans back and sighs with satisfaction*). Lieutenant Tillotson.

The scrape of a chair.

EDWARD (*cannot bear it any longer*). Excuse me.

FATHER. Go on. Go on. Read the next bit.

WILLIAM. Shouldn't I . . . ?

FATHER. Leave the boy alone. Let him sulk. Let him fight his
own battles.

WILLIAM. Yes, but . . . Father.

FATHER. Do as I say, boy. Go on.

JULIA (*getting up*). I'll go.

WILLIAM (*finding the place*). . . . um . . . officer in our land forces . . . .
Father, are you all right?

The parlour.

SISTER JULIAN. He was not all right. The tears were dribbling
down his cheeks. He'd spilled egg yolk on the front of his jacket.
He was going blind. His hands trembled. He was only an old man:
that's all. Nothing more frightening than that. Just an old man.
The pity of it . . . made me cry.

A knock on the door. No answer. JULIA *opens the door.*

JULIA. Edward?

EDWARD (*face muffled in a pillow*). Yes?

JULIA. I just came to see if you . . . I just came to see . . . .

EDWARD (*rolls over and looks at her*). You're crying!

JULIA. No, I'm not.

EDWARD. Because of me?

JULIA. No, because . . . .

EDWARD. You're crying because of me.

JULIA. No, it was your father . . . .

EDWARD. Bloody sadist. No, sorry. I'm sorry. I shouldn't have
sworn. He is though. You saw, didn't you? He did that
deliberately. To humiliate me. To rub it in.

JULIA. He did it because he was so proud.

EDWARD. Proud of William, yes. William this. William bloody that. Blue-eyed soldier-boy William. Three cheers for the blue-eyed soldier-boy. (*Almost in tears.*) What a bloody cheat. Him and not me.

JULIA (*at a loss*). Well, I just . . . I just came to see if there was anything you wanted. (*She starts to leave the room.*)

EDWARD. Julia?

JULIA. Yes?

EDWARD. Will you write to me?

JULIA. Will I . . . ?

EDWARD. I mean when I'm in Switzerland. Will you write to me?

JULIA (*amazed*). Will *I* write to you?

EDWARD. I used to watch you when you were younger. Playing round the pond. Looking for tadpoles. I used to think how pretty your hair was. I still think it's . . . I mean I still watch you sometimes. (*A hint of desperation.*) I don't know what it's like in a sanatorium. I've got to have someone to write to.

JULIA. Yes, all right. If you want.

EDWARD (*head in the pillow again*). You wait. I'll show them. You wait.

Outside in the garden.

WILLIAM (*calling*). Julia!

JULIA. Yes?

WILLIAM (*catching her up*). Have you been up to Edward's room?

JULIA. Yes.

WILLIAM. He won't let me in. He's locked the door. He won't even speak to me.

JULIA. He's very upset.

WILLIAM. I know he's upset. But it's not my fault, is it? There's no reason why he should refuse to speak to *me*.
      Julia . . . at breakfast . . . you were crying, weren't you? Was it because . . . ?

JULIA. It was your father.

WILLIAM. He did that deliberately, you know. It was a rotten thing to do. I feel bad enough about it anyway, without that. I should've refused, shouldn't I? I should've stood up to him. I wonder if I'm not really a bit of a coward. Do you think I am?

JULIA. I don't know.

WILLIAM. No. I suppose not.

JULIA. I don't really know either of you. You're always away.

WILLIAM. I used to watch you sometimes playing all alone in the
garden. I used to wish . . .
Can I tell you something? I'm a bit frightened about all this.
I mean, this commission business. I don't really know if I . . . the
thing is, you see, I thought it'd be Edward and me together. Julia,
do you mind if I write to you? I mean when I'm away. In France
. . . or . . . you know. Would it be all right? Only I think I'll need
to write to someone.

The sounds of war fading into the distance. Hold. A summer afternoon.
MEN *doing odd chores.*

WILLIAM.
Dear Julia,
It's summer here. We're out of the line for three days. Some of
the men are sunbathing. The Germans are about three miles
away. Apparently they're also fighting for King and Country.
Apparently God's on their side as well. When we were in the line,
we could hear them praying . . .

The sounds have faded.

The sanatorium.

EDWARD.
Dear Julia,
The sanatorium is on the side of a mountain. At first I thought
I'd come to a hotel. In the dining-room there's a three-piece
orchestra. They played selections from *Die Fliedermaus* while we
ate and afterwards the consumptives rose from their chairs and
danced among the potted palms. But this morning, I was taken to
the Medical Director's office and the pretence that this was a
hotel was over.

*Sounds used to point the letters where and how necessary. A sense of time
passing.*

WILLIAM.
My dear Julia,
I'm sitting in number 4 trench writing this. Last night in this
section we lost 342 men. It's difficult to remember what for.
I know there were reasons. I think there were. I get in a muddle
now when I try to think. Except if it's about you. I like thinking
about you.

EDWARD.
Dearest Julia,
(*Bitterly:*) My six months period of bed rest is now over. Today,
I tottered in my dressing-gown all the way to the end of the passage.

WILLIAM. Do you ever read the casualty lists in *The Times*? I wonder

if you look at the Ts first. T for Tillotson. A for Arthur. B for
Bellerophon. C for Charlemagne. They're all dead. Roland,
Saladin. Theseus. Here we are stumbling up and down in the mud
over their bodies. They're all here. All blown to pieces. This is the
end of them. You can tell my father that from me if you like.

EDWARD (*bitterly*). How is William? Do you ever hear anything of
him? Still winning medals, I suppose? Still our brave hero? Still
battling through?

Something very private and important to him:

When I was ill, a couple of months ago . . . I had a very high fever,
and I kept dreaming that I was in the desert. Night after night.
Not a dream, a nightmare. I've never had nightmares before.
William had the nightmares. I kept dreaming I was crossing the
desert. The heat was thundering in my head, and then suddenly, it
was night, it was freezing cold and I couldn't close my mouth
because my tongue was so dry and swollen with thirst. I don't
know why I tell you that. Except that it frightens me. I can't get
rid of it.

WILLIAM.
My darling Julia,
    What are you doing now? I sit here for hours dreaming about
you. I imagine you walking in the garden. I make up the
conversations we'll have. We talk about trees and clouds and
water. We have picnics together by the river. We spend whole
afternoons lying on the grass watching the ants and the
butterflies. I know the names of all the wild flowers in the fields
here, (*Reciting dreamily. Hold and fade under* EDWARD.) Common
milkwort, heath bedstraw, tormentil, shepherd's-purse, sun
spurge, cuckooflower . . . .

EDWARD.
My dearest Julia,
    It seems a long time since you last wrote. The doctors say my
lung is completely healed now.
    This is my daily routine: I get up early and run for half an hour.
After breakfast I train with weights and dumb-bells. I am pushing
my body up to and beyond the limits of endurance. Every day
I am able to go a little futher, lift another pound.
    In the evenings I dance with fat, pale ladies from Hamburg.
I pretend I'm dancing with you. I pretend it's the Cafe Royal or
somewhere like that. You and I dancing together . . .

Music fades. A cold wind.

WILLIAM. This was a farmland once . . . when we came here . . .
trees and wheat and cabbages. Men pass through my command
like water through a sieve. Who are they all? I've no idea. I say to

myself: start again from first principles. I am. Start from there. But even that's beyond me now. I am. I *still* am. Why?

The cold wind dies away. Sounds of nuns' voices in chapel. Compline.

The parlour.

TREVOR (*writing, then after a moment*). I had no idea.

SISTER JULIAN. No idea of what?

TREVOR. No idea that Edward Tillotson spent the war in Switzerland. I thought . . . my research so far . . . well, the impression given is that he . . . . Wait a minute . . . where are my notes . . . ?

SISTER JULIAN. He was finally commissioned in August 1918. But it was all more or less over by then. His medical history meant that he was never within a hundred miles of the front line.

TREVOR. I see.

SISTER JULIAN. Whereas William spent almost three years there.

TREVOR (*curious and a little shocked*). And . . . they both wrote to you? These letters . . . ?

SISTER JULIAN. The trouble was, Mr Norman, I was still quite a young girl when they left home . . . 15, 16. I'm afraid I was rather flattered by it all. Letters from a serving officer . . . letters from a consumptive in a Swiss sanatorium. The extremes of romanticism, I thought. I allowed it all to get rather out of hand. I should've seen what was happening and stopped it. But under the circumstances, how could I? What could I say? They needed to write those letters.
I thought: Well, I'll sort it out when Edward's better. I'll sort it out when the war's over. You mustn't imagine I encouraged them. I didn't. There was no need. I wrote very brief, dull letters in reply to theirs. 'Weather here very wet. No eggs.'

TREVOR. And when the war was over?

JULIA. Ah, well . . . . Then . . . .

A room. A number of people gathered.

LAWYER (*fading in*). George Henry Thorndyke Tillotson of Charnwater House in the county of Norfolk, and I hereby revoke all former wills and testamentary dispositions . . . .

The door opens.

JULIA (*entering*). Excuse me. I'm sorry.

LAWYER. Ah, Julia. Come in. Come in. Sit down.

JULIA. I'm sorry I'm so late. The train . . . .

LAWYER. No, no, we've only just started. Thought we might as well begin. (*Resuming the reading of the will.*) Well, now. The smaller legacies first . . . .(*And he continues as below.*)

WILLIAM (*whisper*). Hello, Julia.

EDWARD (*whisper from the other side*). Come and sit here. I've kept you a place.

LAWYER (*carrying straight on over that*). 'To my servant Arthur Durrant the sum of £100. To my servant Dora Barnes, an annuity of £200, the said annuity terminable upon death. To my niece Julia Tillotson, an annuity of £500, to be paid annually by the executors, the said annuity to be terminable upon marriage.' . . . Extraordinary business, that. However . . . 'To my sons Edward John Tillotson and William George Tillotson, the rest of my estate, properties and possessions (*Fading.*) which are to be divided between them as herein stated . . . Charnwater, the house and lands, to be left to my eldest son, Edward; the house in Eaton Square . . . .

Fade up subdued conversation and the noise of glasses.

Well, there we are. If there's any help I can offer you . . . any advice. What are your plans? What will you do now?

WILLIAM. I'm afraid I've no idea.

LAWYER. What about you, Edward?

EDWARD. Oh, I have plans. Yes. I have plans.

WILLIAM. Do they include allowing me to stay here for a bit?

EDWARD. A military hero in my house? Certainly. What an honour. You must do what you want.

WILLIAM. It's not a question of what I want. It's your house now. If you intend to live here then I shall go elsewhere.

EDWARD. I'm planning to go abroad.

WILLIAM. Are you? Then, with your permission, I'll stay here. I'll pay you rent, of course.

LAWYER (*embarrassed at being caught in this flak*). Well, good heavens, I'm sure all this can be sorted out easily enough. What about you, Julia?

JULIA. I don't know. Back to London, I expect.

LAWYER (*drawing her aside*). I must say . . . in confidence . . . I found your uncle's will . . . the clause concerning your annuity . . . very curious. I did my best, but for some reason or other your uncle insisted. (*Fading.*) I don't know whether anything can be done about it . . . .

The garden, EDWARD and JULIA walking.

EDWARD. I've been trying to talk to you alone all afternoon.

JULIA (*who's been avoiding it*). Yes. I know.

EDWARD. It's so good to see you again. It's extraordinary how you've changed.

JULIA. It'd be more extraordinary if I hadn't changed.

EDWARD. Yes, but I remember you differently. When I was in the sanatorium, dancing with you in the evenings, the girl I imagined . . . . Let me look at you.

JULIA (*after a pause*). Are you disappointed?

EDWARD. Your hair's darker than I remembered. You see, Julia, the point is, every time I ran another few yards or lifted a few extra pounds it was for you.

JULIA. Edward, look . . . I think I ought to . . . .

EDWARD (*seriously*). I want to talk to you, Julia.

JULIA. I want to talk to you.

EDWARD. Seriously. About the future.

JULIA. Edward, those letters you wrote . . . .

EDWARD. Did I write to you about the dream I had?

JULIA. Which dream?

EDWARD. The nightmare. I still have it. One version or another. I can't get rid of it. You see, the point is . . . what I'm trying to say, Julia, is that I can't do anything else . . . I can't settle down . . . until I've dealt with it. I have to prove . . . well, I was cheated out of the chance to fight so I haven't proved anything yet. I don't know. I haven't tested myself.
      You do understand, don't you?
      So I thought for the next couple of years . . . . I've been looking at maps, reading a bit . . . there's a whole vast area . . . I don't know if you've heard of it . . . in Southern Arabia. They call it the Empty Quarter, and that's exactly what it is. Literally. It's unmapped desert. But when I come back, Julia . . . assuming that I do come back . . . two, three years perhaps . . . I know it's a long time to expect you to wait. I know it's not fair, but all the same . . .

JULIA (*trying to forestall this*). Edward . . . .

EDWARD. . . . . may I ask you to marry me?

JULIA (*after a pause; distressed*). I don't know. It's very difficult.

EDWARD. I don't see why. What exactly do you mean 'difficult'? The only difficulty I can see is whether you're prepared to wait.

No response.

You do realise, don't you, why my father agreed to make your

annuity terminable upon marriage? So you'd have a reasonable
income until I got back. Then everything will come to you
anyway. As my wife.

JULIA. You mean you discussed this with your father?

EDWARD. Of course we discussed it.

JULIA. Without asking me first! You arranged all this without even
asking me?

EDWARD. Why are you so angry? You're behaving as if there were
nothing at all between us. As if all those letters we wrote to
each other . . . . I thought we had an understanding, you and I.
I thought it was understood . . . (*As she storms off.*) Julia, for
heavens' sake!

The room again.

WILLIAM. Why are you so angry?

JULIA. It's nothing. It's my own fault.

WILLIAM. Julia, may I talk to you for a moment?

JULIA. Not now, William, please. Do you think Durrant would
mind driving me down to the station. Would you ask him?

WILLIAM. You're not leaving already?

JULIA. Yes, I am.

WILLIAM. I thought you were going to stay for a bit.

JULIA. I was, but I've decided I can't.

WILLIAM. I wish you would. It's impossible with Edward here.
We can't stay in the same room together. I've been back for less
than a week, and already . . . .
God! I'm sick to death of his obsessions. Gymnastics out there on
the lawn at six o'clock in the morning. Running up and down
stairs monitoring his pulse rate. Even while my father was dying,
there was Edward checking his own pulse rate. Stay for a little
while. Please.

JULIA. I can't. I've got things to do.

WILLIAM. What things? You don't need to do anything. I think
we've done enough. Too much. We ought to just sit still and
think. We ought to try 'being' for a bit instead of 'doing'. I tell
you what, Julia. When he's gone I'm going to shut those doors
and keep them shut. In the trenches, do you know what I dreamed
of? I dreamed of lying in bed for the rest of my life. Perhaps
I shall. To be freed forever from the necessity of action. To lie
between clean sheets and dream . . . .
    The trouble is I still have nightmares. And then I wake up and
think: why is it so quiet? Are they all dead? Am I the only one left

who isn't dead? The doctors say it's shell shock. Well, it's as good a name as any.

JULIA. Perhaps they're right.

WILLIAM. See how my hands shake? That's guilt. Every minute I expect to be hit. I don't know why the shells and bullets always missed me. Stay and look after me. Make me better.

JULIA. I can't.

WILLIAM. No one else can do it. And when I am better, Julia . . . ?

JULIA (*forestalling him*). No, William. I can't. At least I don't think I can. Not yet anyway.

WILLIAM. I don't mean yet. I know that. But one day.

JULIA (*distressed*). It's very difficult

WILLIAM. No, it isn't. It isn't difficult at all. You just have to remember that I love you. You forget that we've talked together for hours in my head. We've spent whole afternoons together lying on the grass watching the ants and the butterflies. You don't know about all that yet. You don't know what I said to you or what you said to me. I wish you'd stay and let me tell you all about it.

The parlour. The nuns are still singing.

SISTER JULIAN (*lost in thought*). I wonder sometimes what would have happened if I'd stayed. If I'd made a choice then. (*More to* TREVOR:) That was the trouble of course. Making a choice. I didn't want to.

TREVOR. I do think . . . well, it's none of my business, but I do think you ought to have told them. It hardly seems fair, does it?

SISTER JULIAN. Ought to have told them what, Mr Norman?

TREVOR. Well, that they'd . . . that you . . . well, I suppose what I mean is: why didn't you tell them straight out that you didn't love them . . . either of them?

SISTER JULIAN. I don't think you can have been listening properly. Why should I tell them that? I did love them. I loved them both. All those letters. The things they wrote to me. Private things. You don't imagine I was immune to that, do you?

What I tried to tell them, and failed . . . what I think I ought to have made clear to them was that they were deceiving themselves: they didn't love me.

What they loved was their idea of me. They didn't even know me. How can you know somebody who wrote the kind of letters I wrote? They wrote to me about their dreams, and in reply I told them about egg shortages.

The sounds of a small Arabian port.

EDWARD.
Dear Julia,
   Arrived safely in Aden. Negotiating with captain of Arab dhow to take me further on down the coast to Mukalla . . . . (*Fade to silence.*)

WILLIAM.
My darling Julia,
   I have shut all the doors. I've moved into the drawing-room and made myself a nest here . . . a bed and a fire. I've cancelled all the newspapers. I see no one except Dora. The bed's very narrow. Sometimes I lie here with the sheet over my face and think about all those names . . . Privates Acton, Ainsworth, Appleby, Armitage . . . first names . . . then numbers . . . .

This is drowned by the noises of a bustling Arab town.

EDWARD. You'd have been amazed if you'd seen me this afternoon. I sat, dressed in Arab costume, which is much cooler and more practical in this climate . . . I sat, or rather squatted, in the square outside the mosque and bargained with some Bedu tribesmen I've met. Six of them are going to accompany me into the Empty Quarter. They say they know where the wells are. Now it's a matter of organising camels, supplies and guns. They call me *nasrani*, which apparently means 'infidel'. Seems a funny idea to me.

Fading with all the sounds into silence.

WILLIAM (*very quiet*). I lie here looking through the window and watching the seasons change. Things dying away and then budding again and flowering. Worms pulling dead leaves down into the earth. Frogs hopping over the lawn looking for new ponds. I think about this business of survival. It still makes no sense. I still feel I ought to be lying under a field of corn instead of here in this bed.

MEN *talking distantly behind.*

EDWARD. We have eaten our evening meal of rice and dates and now we're drinking coffee round the fire. At night the air is so cold our breath freezes on our beards. But by midday the sun squeezes the skull and almost cracks it open. Sometimes I half lose consciousness and only stay kneeling on my camel by force of habit.

WILLIAM (*out of the silence*). Why do you never come and see me? I'd open the doors for you. You know I would. You should see the trees now . . . white poplar, wych-elm, sweet chestnut, white beam . . .

EDWARD (*interrupting*). What irritates me is that after so much time and effort we only succeeded in going round in circles. I want to get straight across from the Gulf of Aden to the Persian Gulf. From Mukalla to Dhahran. I sail for England on the 14th. Will I see you in London? What are you doing these days? I plan to stay for about two months, deal with business affairs, re-equip myself. And then back again. This time I *will* do it.

WILLIAM. . . . hawthorn, elderberry, dogwood, thorn apple . . . . Edward came for a few days a while ago. He looked very brown and leathery. Did you see him? What the hell are you doing, he said, lying about in bed all the time?

Dora said: 'Don't shout at him. He's got shell-shock.'

I said, 'Edward, I've no idea what I'm doing here. I'm waiting to find out. That's the whole point. Go away and leave me in peace.' It was our birthday while he was here. Dora made a cake. Our birthday. Extraordinary to think we're two halves of the same egg. Why won't you come and see me?

The parlour.

SISTER JULIAN. Because I thought it safer to stay away. And besides, London in the 1920s, even on £500 a year, was tremendous fun. I was enjoying myself. At the back of my mind I knew one day I'd settle down. One day I'd have to choose. But not yet. They were both off on their own separate quests and meanwhile I danced until dawn. I flirted with the idea of other men, but no one else would do. Anyway, it didn't matter yet. There was plenty of time. At least I thought there was, but it's alarming how quickly the time passes when you're enjoying yourself. 1925 . . . 26 . . . 27 . . . .

TREVOR (*stopping her*). Um . . . 1927. That was obviously a very important year.

SISTER JULIAN. Was it?

TREVOR. Well, that was the year Edward finally got through to the Persian Gulf, 900-odd miles across the desert.

SISTER JULIAN. Yes, I believe it was.

TREVOR. I mean, people talk about Scott and Amundsen . . . but as far as I'm concerned . . . I think I've got everything ever written about that expedition.

SISTER JULIAN. Has a lot been written?

TREVOR. Not enough. One thing that bothers me a little . . . 1927 . . . the war had been over . . . what? . . . nine years? Do you mean your cousin William retired to bed for nine years? (*He cannot really believe this.*)

SISTER JULIAN. He wasn't well. He was badly shell-shocked. (*Firmly.*) This is a story, Mr Norman. Listen. I'll tell you what happened next.

JULIA's flat. The phone is ringing. She picks it up.

JULIA (*casually*). Hello? Julia speaking.

DORA (*terrified of the phone*). Hello?

JULIA. Hello?

DORA. Is that you, Miss Julia?

JULIA. Yes.

DORA. It's me. Dora Barnes.

JULIA. Dora! How nice.

DORA. I think you ought to come down here straight away, Miss. It's William.

JULIA. Is he ill?

DORA. He won't let anyone in at all. Not even me. He said: Dora, I want a ladder that'll reach up to the ceiling. Well, I didn't know whether to ring the doctor or not. So then he got quite angry. He said (*panicking:*) Hello?

JULIA. Yes, I'm still here.

DORA. He said: Are you fetching that ladder or not? So Durrant and me, we found a ladder and then soon as he'd got it he shut the door and locked it and he hasn't opened it since. I said to him through the key-hole: What do you want a ladder for, William? But he just laughed and said he was trying to get through to God. Well, that did it, Miss. Me and Durrant thought we ought to ring you . . .

JULIA (*knocking on* WILLIAM's *door*). William!

WILLIAM (*muffled*). Who is it?

JULIA. It's me. Julia.

WILLIAM (*hardly believing it*). Julia?

JULIA. Open the door. Will you please open this door at once or we'll break in though the window.

The door opens.

WILLIAM (*happily*). Julia. How wonderful. What are you doing here?

JULIA. Dora sent for me. She seems to think you've finally gone mad.

WILLIAM. I haven't gone mad. Quite the opposite.

JULIA. I must say, you don't look particularly mad. You look very well.

WILLIAM. I am very well.

JULIA. What's all this about a ladder? She says . . . .

WILLIAM. Do you remember the story of Esau and Jacob? 'And the first came out red like an hairy garment. And after that came his brother out?' I was thinking about Jacob's ladder reaching all the way up to heaven.

No, actually . . . I was lying here looking up at the ceiling and I suddenly had this urge to paint it. Which may be the same thing. Do you think so?

JULIA. It does look a bit shabby.

WILLIAM. No, no, I mean to *paint* it. To paint *on* it. I've made a design up there in pencil . . . of leaves and sky. I thought I'd make it so that when you looked up you'd think you were in a forest.

JULIA. *Can* you paint?

WILLIAM. I don't know yet. Well, no, literally I can't because I haven't got any paints.

You could send me some from London, couldn't you? Or better still bring them. I'll write you a list of what I want.

Come and see what I've done up there. Climb up and look.

Perhaps I'll paint the walls too. With tree trunks and grass, and I'll have squirrels and deer, and birds up in the leaves, and rabbits.

JULIA. Why did you lock the doors? Dora was worried.

WILLIAM. I didn't want anybody disturbing me until it was clear in my mind. You can leave them open now though. It doesn't matter. I shan't shut them again unless it's cold. I don't need to anymore. You shouldn't frown like that. Come on. Let's go out for a walk.

JULIA (*amazed*). Out? You want to go out?

WILLIAM. It's time I did. I want to look at the trees close up.

JULIA. All right.

WILLIAM. I shall have all kinds of flowers in my forest. Windflowers and wood sorrel and primroses. In fact I might paint flowers all over the floor. Yes, I will. And ants and butterflies. Do you think I need a coat?

JULIA. Yes, I do. And something on your feet.

WILLIAM. Will you stay here and come for walks with me every day and make sure I've got my coat on?

JULIA. I can't do that. You know I can't. I've got things to do in London.

WILLIAM. You always say that. You always say you've got things to do.

JULIA. Well, so I have.

WILLIAM. What things?

JULIA. I don't know. Just things.

WILLIAM. I should've thought you'd done them all by now. I'd be sick to death of them if I were you. Aren't you ready to settle down yet? I think you are. You look tired. See . . . I can't smooth away the frown. Why don't you come and rest here. Why don't you marry me?

JULIA (*with exasperated tenderness*). You can't even do your buttons up straight.

WILLIAM (*very close*). Will you?

JULIA. I don't know.

WILLIAM. You did say . . . when I was better . . . you did agree . . . .

JULIA. I don't think I did. I think you . . . .

WILLIAM. And now I am better.

JULIA. It's so difficult.

WILLIAM. That's what you said last time I asked.

JULIA. You hardly know me.

WILLIAM. How can you say that! I've known you all my life. I love you.

JULIA. Yes, but what would we *do*?

WILLIAM. What do you mean what would we do? We wouldn't do anything. I'd paint you in a white dress coming through the woods with a basket of flowers.

JULIA. No, you don't understand . . . I couldn't live here and do nothing.

WILLIAM. I wonder if I could paint you. I've only been thinking about trees up to now. Do you remember that conversation you and I had about painting trees?

JULIA. Painting . . . ?

WILLIAM. And you said something about Renoir and light.

JULIA. I never said anything about Renoir and light.

WILLIAM. Yes, you did.

JULIA. I don't know anything about Renoir. We've never had a conversation about trees.

WILLIAM. Yes, we have.

JULIA. We can't have done. I didn't even know you were interested in painting.

WILLIAM. You did.

JULIA. No, I didn't. This is the first I've heard about it.

WILLIAM. But we've often talked about it.

JULIA. William, we haven't.

WILLIAM. Hundreds of times.

JULIA. When? Name one.

WILLIAM. Oh, years ago. When we were walking by the river.

JULIA. When? We've never walked by a river. This is all in your head.

WILLIAM. No, it isn't. I . . . .

JULIA. Yes, it is. You see! You don't know anything about me. Nothing at all. You lie around and dream all day. Everything that happens in your head.

WILLIAM. Some of it, yes. But that doesn't mean . . . .

JULIA. I can't marry a man . . . I mean look at you! What a mess you are . . . odd shoes . . . your buttons done up crooked . . . your hair . . . .

WILLIAM. You think I'm a mess?

JULIA. And this room. The curtains are torn. Look at the dust. The filth. Writing all over the walls. Scribbling on the ceiling.

WILLIAM. It's not scribbling.

JULIA. It looks like scribbling. I couldn't cope with all this. And how long since anything's been done to the house? The garden's a wilderness.

WILLIAM. That's how I like it.
    I suppose you'd prefer it if I was more like Edward. Rushing round the world trying to conquer the elements. Is that what you admire?

JULIA. At least he does something. At least he does something concrete.

WILLIAM. I expect one day that's literally what he'll do. Start tearing down the forests and covering them all with concrete.

JULIA. At least he goes out and fights. He doesn't run away.

WILLIAM. Is that what you think of me?

JULIA. Yes, that is what I think.

WILLIAM. Perhaps I did dream you then. My Julia never thought that. My Julia knew better.

Sounds of the desert. Men's voices.

EDWARD. This evening the sand is rose-coloured . . . and in the distance gold . . . and beyond that purple. I love the desert. I love the emptiness of it. The space. You have no idea how beautiful it is . . . how clean . . . how untouched . . . .
    The journey back from the Gulf is proving more difficult than

I anticipated. My friends the Bedu all went about their private
affairs in Dhahran, and the men I have travelling with me now are
from another tribe. I can't say I altogether trust them.

I hope you've written to me. I hope there are letters waiting for
me in Aden. I want to know everything you've been doing.

The parlour

SISTER JULIAN. What was I doing? This and that. Dancing. Going
out to supper. Enjoying myself. But, for some reason or other,
I was beginning to get a little bored with it. A little tired of having
fun. Or rather, what had seemed like fun. I thought . . . walking
home along streets where newsboys called out the headlines . . .
perhaps William's right. Perhaps it is time to settle down.

The desert.

EDWARD (*in some physical distress*). I wonder if you'll ever receive this
letter. I'm writing it with the stump of a pencil on the back pages
of my note book. They've stolen everything else. I never trusted
them. Black teeth and treacherous smiles. Two days ago . . .
I think two days ago . . . we arrived at the well we'd been
searching for, but some other men were already there. My men
recognised them. Apparently the two tribes are involved in some
kind of feud . . . something to do with the theft of some camels.
My men tried to run away. I said, 'Now look here, if there's a
legitimate quarrel, then you should sort it out. Stand your
ground.' But they decided this was further proof that Allah was
angry with them for travelling with a *nasrani*.

While I was sleeping, they stole away, taking the camels, the
guns and all our supplies with them.

How long ago was that? I've lost track of time. They took my
watch and my compass and my water carrier. And after all this,
the well was dry. My tongue . . . almost impossible to swallow . . .
If I die now, how long will it take for the flesh to be picked clean
from my bones and the bones to dry up and crumble away. Dust
blown about by wind, trickling through the sand. No one will
ever know.

Not strong enough, Julia.

(*Hardly able to speak.*) Beaten . . . .

JULIA's *flat. The phone rings.*

JULIA. Hello. Holborn 4192.

WOMAN. Miss Julia Tillotson?

JULIA. Yes.

WOMAN. I have a cable here for you, Miss Tillotson. From a
Mr John McCleod.

JULIA. I don't know a John McCleod.

WOMAN. Is that Miss Julia Tillotson, Holborn 4192, Flat B.
24, Fitzalan Street . . . ?

JULIA. Yes, but who is . . . ?

WOMAN. The cablegram was sent from somewhere called Alhakran
. . . is that right . . . cabled through from Aden. August 3. It reads:
Edward Tillotson seriously ill. Advise immediate presence.
Contact John McCleod, Hotel Al Haruf. Alhakhran . . . .

Arab hospital.

JULIA. Edward?

EDWARD. Mmm?

JULIA. Are you awake?

EDWARD (*coming to*). Julia!

JULIA (*bursting into tears*). Oh, Edward!

EDWARD. Good Lord, there's no need to start snivelling.

JULIA. You're going to be all right?

EDWARD. Of course I'm going to be all right.

JULIA (*trying to pull herself together*). I couldn't find you. I tried to
contact this John McCleod person but he wasn't there. And
I couldn't find . . . I thought maybe . . . Oh, Edward, this is an
awful place.

EDWARD. Did you get my letters?

JULIA (*not on this line of thought at all*). What letters?

EDWARD. I wrote you pages and pages all in blunt pencil.
Explaining what happened. It was my dream. My nightmare. And
I survived it. You can't imagine . . . the ultimate test . . . and here
I am. I survived.

JULIA. I thought . . . when I got the cable . . . I was afraid I'd be
too late.

EDWARD. Good Lord, no. You don't get rid of me as easily as that.
Couple of cracked ribs now. That's all.

JULIA. What happened?

EDWARD. I told you. It was my nightmare in every particular.
No water . . . the heat . . . .
I'm glad you're here. I asked McCleod to send you a cable.

JULIA. Who is this McCleod?

EDWARD. Friend of mine.

JULIA. He said you were seriously ill. I thought you were dying.

EDWARD (*amused*). Me? Dying? Listen, do you remember the pond at Charnwater? In the garden? Do you remember when I went in after the cricket ball? I was thinking about that, lying in the sand hallucinating about water. I was thinking about all that frog spawn, the thousands of tadpoles that failed to hatch out or got eaten. The hundreds of frogs that got taken by birds or trodden on or run over. The handful that survived. The one that turned into a prince. That seems to me a fundamental principle. Don't you think so?

JULIA. Edward, these sheets are filthy. We ought to get you out of here.

EDWARD. Those who survive deserve to do so simply by virtue of the fact that they have survived. No matter how. The fundamental principle of nature. I think we ought to accept that . . . it's not something we should ignore.

JULIA. How soon can we get you home?

EDWARD (*surprised*). Home?

JULIA. Back to England.

EDWARD. I'm not going back to England. Good Lord no. Whatever made you think that? (*Having looked at her properly.*) What have you done with your hair?

JULIA. I haven't done anything with my hair.

EDWARD. Yes, you have. It's brown.

JULIA. It's always been brown.

EDWARD. No it hasn't. It was a sort of golden colour. Long golden hair. That's how I remember it.

JULIA. You must be thinking of someone else. Some other woman.

EDWARD. No, I'm not. I've never in my life thought about any other woman but you. Not seriously.

JULIA (*moved*). Is that true?

EDWARD. You know it's true.

A silent, very close moment.

I said when all this was over . . . when I'd got it out of my system . . . I'd ask you to marry me.

JULIA (*agreeing with him*). Yes.

A kiss.

The door opens. McCLEOD *enters.*

EDWARD. Ah, here he is. Come in. Come in. Let me introduce you. This is John McCleod . . .

McCLEOD. Look, I'm sorry. I'm interrupting. I just . . .

EDWARD. . . . and this is my cousin, Julia Tillotson.

JULIA. I must thank you for letting me know about Edward.

McCLEOD. Sorry I wasn't at the hotel when you arrived. They said a Miss Tillotson had been asking for me so I thought I'd better check you'd found the place. It isn't easy to find. Not very prepossessing once you've found it, either. Well, look, I'll come back in an hour or two if that's all right. Business, Miss Tillotson. Your cousin and I have plans. (*Leaving.*) Perhaps I'll see you at the hotel later.

EDWARD. Splendid fellow McCleod. He and I are going into business together.

JULIA. Yes, what sort of business?

EDWARD. Oil.

JULIA. Oil! Do you know anything about oil?

EDWARD. Not a thing. But he does. Hell of a lot. He's been out here doing a bit of private prospecting. It was his camp I came floundering into, stumbling and flapping over a ridge of sand, yelling some delirious nonsense or other. They nearly shot me. Thought I was a mad Arab. Thought I was about to go beserk with a rifle and wipe them all out. Do you know, Julia, that under this desert is enough oil to flood the whole of Europe? In ten years, you look out of that window and there'll be oil wells as far as the eye can see . . . from here to Bahrain. We'll be as rich as Croesus.

JULIA. Who'll be as rich as Croesus?

EDWARD. We will. You and me and McCleod.

JULIA. You're going to sink oil wells all over the desert?

EDWARD. *We* are. A partnership. I'm putting up the bulk of the capital . . . .

JULIA. You mean oil wells all over the desert! You can't do that!

EDWARD. Yes I can. You wait.

JULIA. You can't.

EDWARD. Why not?

JULIA. After everything you wrote? All those letters? Your desert. The emptiness. The space. How clean it is. How beautiful. Untouched, you said. Rose and gold. You can't fill it full of machinery and shanty towns and speculators and oil pipes.

EDWARD (*cool*). Why can't I?

JULIA. Well, because you can't! Why would you want to? What are you doing it for?

EDWARD. What for? Because the whole idea of it excites me. Oil, Julia. Think of it. Busines. Money. A kind of war. Strategy. Tactics. Opening up new fronts. Establishing new front lines. Making sudden unexpected moves. Taking prisoners. The winners. The losers. The casualties. I want to know if I can survive. I want to be the winner. We're going to make a fortune out of this.

JULIA. What do you want to make a fortune for? You've got money. You've got enough. You don't need any more.

EDWARD. Don't be ridiculous, Julia. Everybody wants more.

JULIA. I didn't say want.

EDWARD. Anyone who claims he doesn't is a liar or a fool.

JULIA. William doesn't want more.

EDWARD (*exasperated*). For God's sake, how do you suppose William would manage if someone in the past . . . some ancestor . . . hadn't made a fortune out of something or the other? You can't be as self-indulgent as William is unless somebody's made the money for you. And that's another thing. Money makes money. Look around you. Look at this hospital. In twenty years these Arabs'll be so stinking rich this hospital will be a miracle of cleanliness . . . all the latest medical techniques. You can't live on the past forever.

JULIA. Yes, but . . . .

EDWARD. The point is do they have the skills to find the oil themselves? Do they have the skills to raise foreign capital? No, they don't. So somebody will have to do it for them. And if I'm prepared to risk everything I've got . . . .
      Look, you can't be sentimental about these things, Julia. You can't stand in the way of progress.

JULIA. Yes, but is it progress? How do you know it is?

EDWARD. Of course it's progress. What's the matter with you? Obviously it's progress.
      I thought you'd be as excited as I am about it all. I was going to get McCleod to drive us out to the camp in a couple of days. I was going to show you where we hope to start drilling. Good Lord, Julia, a man expects a certain amount of support from his wife.

JULIA. I can't do it.

EDWARD. Where are you going? Sit down.

JULIA. It's a mistake. I can't possibly marry you.

EDWARD. Of course you can. It's all fixed. Oh, for goodness sake, I can't stand temperamental women. What do you *want* me to do?

(*Calling after her.*) Where are you going?

JULIA (*calling back*). Away!

The parlour.

TREVOR (*after a moment*). It's gone very quiet. Have you noticed?
They stopped singing a while ago.

SISTER JULIAN. It's the Great Silence.

TREVOR (*alarmed*). The Great . . . ?

SISTER JULIAN. It only means that the rule of our order prohibits
us from speaking until early tomorrow morning.

TREVOR. Then shouldn't you . . . I mean, should I . . . ?

SISTER JULIAN. I haven't finished yet. This is far more important
than observing the rule. Listen. I did precisely what I said I'd do.
I went away. And I stayed away. For years. How can I explain this
to you?
   You see, until then, Mr Norman, I'd lived entirely on instinct.
Rather like a moth caught between two lights, fluttering between
them. Yes, very like a moth. As unthinking and as silly. I fluttered
about, uncertain where to settle, bruising and burning myself but
quite incapable of flying away into the darkness. And there I was,
thirty years old, certain that the time had finally come to choose,
and yet when I took a closer look I saw that I couldn't possibly
marry either of them. For one thing, they were both impossible;
for another, how dangerous to throw one's weight behind this
one rather than that: how dangerous to choose. I must go away,
I thought. I didn't know what else to do. I'd always assumed, you
see, that in the end I'd marry one or other of them. It was just a
matter of deciding which. They should never have been two
people at all. They should have been one. One man. And what an
extraordinary man that would have been. He'd have been worth
writing about. And I could have married that man. As it was, the
farther away I went the better.

TREVOR. Where did you go?

SISTER JULIAN. Oh, all over the place. Australia. South America.
Borneo. The Philippines. Looking. Weighing things up. And
finally I settled in Bali. A beautiful place. You could live there
simply and honestly. Let them get on with it, I thought.

WILLIAM.
   My dearest Julia,
      Happy Christmas. Hope you like the card. You know that dark
passageway from the stableyard to the kitchen. I've painted a view
of open fields on both sides. Stalks of barley, shoulder high . . .
cornflowers, poppies, harvest mice . . . .

EDWARD.
McTill Oil, Alhakhran.
My dear Julia,
   The first pipeline is now through to the Gulf and fully
operational. This is going to make things considerably easier and
much faster. McCleod is working about 50 miles north of here:
we hope to have two new drilling rigs in action by the end of
the year.

WILLIAM. One of Edward's lawyers turned up yesterday. Some
estate papers for me to sign. Did you know that this company of
his . . . McTill Oil or whatever they call themselves . . . have gone
into shipping now? I imagine fleets of McTill Oil tankers steaming
through the Suez Canal. First the desert. Now the sea. What
next? When are you coming home? It's years since I saw you . . . .

EDWARD. I don't know whether you get newspapers out there, but
my impression is that the situation in Europe is rapidly
deteriorating. My advice is to come home as soon as possible.

WILLIAM. Insurance. International Finance. What is he not
involved in? The latest thing apparently is land speculation. He's
buying up land in South America for the mineral rights. Burning
down the jungles. Building roads . . . .

EDWARD. Julia, it's no good saying you'll be a lot safer where you
are. The trouble isn't going to confine itself to Europe. The
chances are you'll be considerably worse off where you are.
Besides, in times of trouble . . . anyway, time you came back.
I've arranged for money to be wired through to you for your
passage home . . . .

WILLIAM. . . . on one side of the bathroom passage I have painted
the sea, and on the other side sand dunes. You walk along the
water's edge past baby crabs and bladderwrack . . . and on the
ceiling herring gulls with silvery fish in their beaks.

EDWARD. Did you have any idea what William was up to at
Charnwater? The whole house, apparently . . . is covered in
paintings. The walls . . . the floors. And stacks of canvasses all
over the place. 'Any of it worth putting on the market,' I asked.
But the lawyers say no. Just amateurish daubs. Pity really. Ruin
of a life.

WILLIAM. . . . a huge canvas. Of a garden. A wild, tangled garden
full of honeysuckle. I'm wondering whether or not to include a
figure in it. I'm not very good at figures. Put one in and the
thing's ruined. Perhaps I could make it an angel with a flaming
sword barring the gates.

LAWYER.
Tillotson and McCleod International Ltd.
McTill House, London W1.
Dear Miss Tillotson,
   I am instructed by Mr Edward Tillotson to inform you that a
passage has been booked for you on the SS *Princess Adelaide* sailing
from Singapore on October 7. I am further instructed to inform
you that in future the payment of your annuity will be dependent
on your personal signature witnessed here in our London Office.
We look forward . . . .

EDWARD. Of course I have the right. I'm executor of the will.
Do as you're told and come home at once.

A restaurant.

WAITER. This way, Madam . . . Mr Tillotson's waiting for you.

JULIA (*coolly*). Hello, Edward.

EDWARD (*as they sit*). Bring us a couple of dry martinis. We'll order
in a minute.

WAITER. Very good, sir. (*He goes.*)

JULIA. Well, here I am. I did as I was told.

EDWARD. It's not a matter of doing what you're told. It's a matter
of common sense.

JULIA. Common sense? Oh really? I'd call it blackmail.

EDWARD. You'll be a good deal safer here than you would be in
the Far East. You wait and see. I know what I'm talking about.

The WAITER *returns with the drinks.*

Ah . . . thank you.

WAITER. And the menu, sir, madam.

JULIA. Thank you.

EDWARD. And if things should heat up here then we'll send you off
to America. Should be safe enough there.

JULIA. I don't want to go to America. I'm going back to Bali as
soon as I've unravelled whatever legal knots you've tied round
my money.

EDWARD. Well now, what shall we have to start with? What about
a little smoked salmon?

JULIA. I'm not all that fond of smoked salmon.

EDWARD. It's very good here. I think you'll like it. And then we
might try the Canard au Poivre. (*As they examine the menu.*) When
the bombing starts we'll send you down to Charnwater. You can
look after William for a bit.

JULIA. You're very fond of sending people about the place, aren't you?

EDWARD. For your own safety.

JULIA. Like a parcel. I suppose I must look rather like one. I haven't got the kind of clothes you wear to a place like this.

EDWARD. You look splendid.

JULIA. No, I don't.

EDWARD. Older, of course. But then we're all older. As a matter of fact, it'd be a good idea if William had someone else beside Dora living there for a while. Apparently he's as mad as a hatter these days.

JULIA (*coldly*). Have you seen him recently?

EDWARD. Haven't seen him in years. We don't get on all that well, William and I. Still, now I'm in England for a bit . . . . (*Sudden idea.*) Tell you what, why don't we both go down to Charnwater the week after next? For Christmas. Have a proper English Christmas.

JULIA (*suddenly wanting to*). I suppose we could.

EDWARD (*gently*). Your hair's going grey. There.

JULIA. So's yours. There.

EDWARD. Ten years. It's too long, Julia. I should have fetched you home long ago.

SISTER JULIAN (*remembering*). The road from the station was lined on either side with new semi-detached houses . . . red brick houses with mock-Tudor garages. Like scabs. Oh yes, the taxi driver said, the developers are moving in now. There's money to be made in that line of business. People commute into Norwich now. They're building in the field behind the church as well. 'People must live somewhere,' I said. I know that. He stopped off for petrol at the bottom of Charn Lane. There was a brand new garage there. It's all progress, the taxi driver said. Yes, I suppose it must be.

The taxi. Hold under:

And then he turned into the drive. The gates were broken and unpainted. The drive was ankle-deep in weeds. The trees pressed up against the side windows . . . .

The taxi stops.

WILLIAM. How wonderful it is to see you. Come in . . . come out of the cold . . . come and sit by the fire . . . .

JULIA (*passing from outside to inside with the door closing behind her*). It's like walking from one wild garden to another. From a winter garden to a summer garden.

WILLIAM (*pleased by her reaction*). Do you like it? In the gun room I'm painting a jungle . . . you should see that. (*Slightly uneasy.*) Where's Edward? Isn't he with you?

JULIA. He's coming by car. I thought he'd be here before me. He's been over to Liverpool. Somewhere near there. Inspecting a site for a new refinery.

WILLIAM. Hasn't he got enough refineries?

A car coming up the drive, very distant as yet.

Come and sit by the fire. Your hands are so cold. (*Calling.*) Dora! Julia's here. (*To* JULIA.) Would you like some tea?

JULIA. Is that a car?

WILLIAM (*beginning to panic*). Is it?

JULIA. That'll be him.

WILLIAM (*nervous*). Wait . . . I haven't seen him since . . . I don't know when.

The car has drawn up, stopped. The sound of its doors, etc.

Not for years. I don't know if I can face this.

JULIA. Don't let him bully you.

EDWARD (*calling from outside the front door*). Hello? Anybody home? Do I have to ring the bell?

JULIA. He will if he can. Don't let him.

WILLIAM. I don't know if I . . . wait . . . wait . . . . (*As* JULIA *goes to open the door.*)

EDWARD (*opening it himself*). There you are! Happy Christmas.

WILLIAM (*very moved*). Edward . . . .

EDWARD (*equally so*). William . . . Good Lord.

The dining-room. General chatter.

EDWARD. A toast. I propose a toast. To us! Together again.

ALL. To us. Happy Christmas (*etc.*).

EDWARD. Your very good health.

WILLIAM. I've eaten too much. Have to start undoing some buttons.

EDWARD. You're getting fat, William.

JULIA. Why not? It suits him.

WILLIAM. People will be able to tell us apart now. The fat one and the lean one.

EDWARD. I doubt if they have any difficulty doing that anymore. You've let yourself go, William. Look at all this.

WILLIAM (*embarrassed*). Don't.

JULIA. Don't prod him.

EDWARD. You should keep yourself in better shape. It's like the house. Look at the state you've let the house get into.

WILLIAM. It's how I like it.

EDWARD. Twenty years of neglect. The poor place is falling down.

WILLIAM. There's everything here. Forests. Fields. The sea . . . .

JULIA. Gardens. Jungles. It's quite extraordinary. I've never seen anything like it.

EDWARD. The point is though it's been so damn neglected. Dry rot . . . wet rot. I was having a look at the roof this morning . . . .

WILLIAM. It's how I like it.

EDWARD. Yes, but it isn't your house, is it? Best thing to do now is to get a surveyor in. See whether it's worth putting to rights or not.

WILLIAM (*alarmed*). What do you mean 'putting to rights or not'? (*To* JULIA:) What does he mean?

EDWARD. That's the trouble with your lot.

WILLIAM. My lot?

JULIA. What do you mean 'his lot'?

EDWARD. Leave you in charge of anything and what happens? The whole damned thing falls to pieces. And you sit around like Nero . . . there's an example for you . . . fiddling or painting pictures or whatever, while the structure tumbles round your ears. After which, of course, somebody has to come along . . . somebody like me . . . to clear up the mess and get things running smoothly again.

JULIA. Yes, I could give you some historical examples as well . . . the sort of person who comes along to clear up the mess.

EDWARD. I think William can answer for himself, Julia.

JULIA. Oh, I'm sorry. I hadn't realised you'd asked him a question. I thought this was a general conversation.

EDWARD (*annoyed, to* JULIA). I don't know why . . . .

WILLIAM (*trying to make peace*). Who wants another chocolate?

A pause.

EDWARD. I think what we need is some fresh air. Bit of exercise. Come on. A good long walk. What about you, Dora?

JULIA. Dora is going to put her feet up by the fire.

EDWARD (*moving away*). Come on. Coats. Boots. Gloves. Do you good, William. Get some of that fat off. (*Going.*) Pity there are no dogs here these days . . . .

JULIA *and* WILLIAM, *slightly under their breath, like conspirators.*

JULIA. You mustn't let him bully you.

WILLIAM. What did he mean? About the house? Whether it's worth putting to rights or not?

JULIA. You never used to let him bully you. Perhaps if we stick together, you and I.

WILLIAM. It's true though, isn't it? The house *is* falling down. I hadn't noticed. I don't think about it. But he's probably right.

JULIA (*trying to put fighting spirit into* WILLIAM). Then *he* can repair it.

WILLIAM. But from what he said . . . he made it sound . . . .

JULIA. What's the point of making all that money if you don't use it for the things that matter?

WILLIAM. Bits of paint on a wall. I don't know if they do matter, except to me.

JULIA. They're not just bits of paint on a wall. You know they're not. You *know* what they are.

EDWARD (*calling*). Come on . . . hurry up!

EDWARD, JULIA *and* WILLIAM *are walking down the drive.*

. . . the point is, Julia, we won't be able to rely on the shipping lanes staying open. For a start, they'll blockade the Channel . . . .

WILLIAM (*slightly distant*). Look at the sun, Julia.

EDWARD (*breaking wood*). Damn branches. (*Calling slightly.*) Why don't you have them cut back?

JULIA. You'll volunteer, will you, this time?

EDWARD. Well . . . 42, you know. Probably too old for active service. But yes . . . naturally I'll volunteer.

WILLIAM. Nothing natural about it.

EDWARD. Ah yes . . . well, you say that because your philosophy of life . . . if you have one . . . fails to take into account observable biological fact. We can't deny what we are. Red in tooth and claw. The survival of the fittest.

JULIA. The princess and the frog. Remember that one? The thousands that got trodden on or run over or eaten by birds . . . thousands of expendable frogs . . . the handful that survive . . . the one that turns into a prince.

WILLIAM. I always thought that story meant that people need beautiful things round them otherwise they can't ever be truly themselves. Or maybe that everybody has the potential . . . .

EDWARD. Careful! That's the edge of the pond.

WILLIAM. It's all right. It's solid ice under the snow.

JULIA. Will it hold?

EDWARD. Be careful, Julia.

JULIA (*at a distance*). I'm the lightest.

WILLIAM (*to himself*). Look at the frost on the reeds.

JULIA (*stamping*). It's as thick as anything. (*Trying to slide.*) Anyway, perhaps there won't be a war.

EDWARD. There will.

JULIA. How do you know? Anything could happen.

EDWARD. No way of stopping it. One of our subsidiaries has just negotiated a loan for the German government. People talk. One hears things. We've a number of contacts in Germany. Steel, for example. Considerable holdings in Krupp's steel. Can't help noticing which way the wind's blowing.

JULIA (*appalled*). You mean, you're going to make profits out of . . . ? You're going to profit . . . ?

EDWARD (*shrugging*). Two refineries in Germany, one in Austria. One has to keep one's ear to the ground.

JULIA. You can't lose, can you!

EDWARD. Yes, of course we can lose. However, if we spread our interests as widely as possible. We're an international company, Julia. It's difficult to avoid profiting by whatever the international situation happens to be. That's what we do. That's the point. We make profits.

JULIA. Are you listening to this, William?

WILLIAM. I was just thinking of going to look for some skates.

EDWARD. It's no good being naive about money, Julia.

JULIA (*outraged*). And then you say you're going to volunteer. I mean, with one hand . . . .

EDWARD. You mustn't confuse patriotism with profit. War won't bring the world to an end. War's simply a cleansing mechanism. It has its uses. But without profits then we should be in trouble.

WILLIAM (*bravely*). I'd have thought that on the contrary . . . .

EDWARD. Where are those skates you were talking about.

Sense that EDWARD *has tried sliding and moved away from them.*

JULIA (*to* WILLIAM, *urging him on*). That's right. Say it. Answer him. On the contrary . . . . Go on!

WILLIAM (*miserably*). I don't know. I can't answer him, Julia.

EDWARD (*from a distance*). Do you know I'd forgotten all about those fields over there. What do you use them for?

WILLIAM. I don't use them for anything.

EDWARD. We don't rent them out, do we?

WILLIAM (*sense that he slides across to join* EDWARD). I let the farmer down the road have the grass if he wants it.

EDWARD. How much does he give you for it?

WILLIAM. Nothing. If he wants it he's welcome to it. I don't need it.

EDWARD. No wonder your financial affairs are in such a mess. (*An idea.*) You know, if we were to bring an access road through from Charn Lane, we could build in those fields. What? Twenty, thirty houses? There's a lot of building going on round here. (*The idea developing.*) We could bring the road along that side of the pond and build say another ten . . . maybe twelve detached houses with garages . . . .

WILLIAM. Ten detached houses in this garden? In my garden?

EDWARD. If we knocked down the old house we could probably fit twelve in.
     My garden, actually.

JULIA. But you're not going to knock down the old house. You're going to repair it.

EDWARD. I doubt it'd be worth the outlay.

WILLIAM (*panicking; to* JULIA). He can't knock it down. He can't do that, can he?

EDWARD. No use throwing good money after bad. It's not as if it's a particularly beautiful house.

WILLIAM. But all my paintings . . .

EDWARD. If we demolished it, we'd have a very commercial proposition on our hands.

JULIA. You keep saying 'we'. *We* don't want the house demolished. It's unique. One day it'll be worth thousands. Hundreds of thousands, if that's what matters.

EDWARD. I doubt that. Amateurish daubs.

JULIA. Who says amateurish daubs?
     William, for God's sake say something. (*Sudden desperate decision.*) Listen. William and I have something to tell you. We wanted to keep it a secret, but now . . . .

EDWARD (*amused*). A secret?

JULIA (*desperately bluffing*). Shall I tell him or will you?

WILLIAM (*at sea*). What?

JULIA (*deep breath*). William and I are getting married. And we want to buy Charnwater. Sell it to us.

EDWARD. Don't be absurd. You've neither of you got two pennies to rub together. I should know.

JULIA. Then *give* it to us. As a wedding present.

EDWARD (*slightly unnerved*). What is this? Some joke? What are you playing at? Good God, if it means that much to you, Julia, have Charnwater. Take it. You don't have to pretend you want to marry a washed-up buffoon like William . . . .

JULIA. Don't let him call you that!

WILLIAM. He's probably right.

JULIA. He isn't right! For heaven's sake! William is an artist.

EDWARD. William is a lazy, gutless fool. Look at him. (*He prods* WILLIAM.)

JULIA. Don't do that.
    If you really want to know, William and I have been engaged for years.

EDWARD. Nonsense. (*Another prod.*)

WILLIAM. Don't.

JULIA. He asked me to marry him twenty years ago. Didn't you? Tell him.

EDWARD. If you're engaged to anyone, you're engaged to me.

JULIA. I've never been engaged to you!

EDWARD. A dirty hospital room in Alhakhran? I asked you then and you said yes.

JULIA. I did not say yes. I nearly did but in the end I didn't.

EDWARD. All right, I thought, let her have her head for a few years if that's what she wants. Oh, for God's sake, Julia. I'm 42. You're nearly 40. If we don't do something about it soon, it'll be too late. Look, forget about Charnwater. It's yours. Give it to William if that's what all this is about. Do what you want with it.

JULIA. That's not the point.

EDWARD. Then what is?

JULIA. The point is I want to marry William.

EDWARD. No you don't. You're saying that to annoy me. Nobody with a grain of sense could see this lump of flab (*Prod.*) as a serious proposition.

WILLIAM. Stop doing that. Leave me alone.

EDWARD. Ah, he can speak, can he! (*A vicious prod.*)

WILLIAM. Stop it.

EDWARD. Great bag of jelly. Look at that. (*And again.*)

JULIA. Hit him back. Go on. Hit him.

EDWARD. Let's see what you can do, then. Apart from daubing paint all over the place. Apart from making a mess of every bloody wall in the house . . .

JULIA. Don't let him push you about. Hit him. (WILLIAM *does.*)

EDWARD. That's more like it. (*Dodging a punch.*) Ah, look . . . we've got him angry now . . . . That's the way. Is this (*Punch.*) what you want to marry, Julia? This (*Punch.*) . . . this (*Punch.*) . . . .

The noise of them fighting. Then the ice cracking.

JULIA (*screaming over the noise*). Watch out! The ice! Move!

The ice cracks. Cries and gasps as the MEN *fall into the water. Splashing; splintering.* JULIA's *reaction.*

SISTER JULIAN (*narrating*). I stood there . . . quite frozen . . . watching them slide into the water. Still locked together. Still struggling. They said afterwards that William died immediately. Of shock. I remember his eyes opening wide as if he couldn't believe what was happening. At the inquest they said his heart wasn't strong. The legacy of the war, they said. And Edward . . . .

EDWARD. Julia! For God's sake . . . your hand . . . help me . . . .

SISTER JULIAN (*narrating*). I stood staring at him.

EDWARD. Julia!

SISTER JULIAN (*narrating*). His hands flailed about in the air.

EDWARD. Your scarf . . . .

SISTER JULIAN (*narrating*). And at last he managed to heave his arms over the edge of the firm ice and clutch at my ankles.

JULIA. No!

EDWARD. For God's sake help me!

SISTER JULIAN (*narrating*). My feet slid from under me. I fell. He held on. Pulling me in. And I kicked and kicked until I'd kicked his hands away and there was nothing for him to hang on to.

EDWARD (*his mouth filling with water*). For God's sake, get help . . . .

The bubbling as he goes under.

Silence.

SISTER JULIAN (*narrating*). And then suddenly Dora was there, dragging the ladder behind her, pushing me out of the way, leaning over the edge and grabbing Edward's wrists. The opportunity was gone.

We are in the parlour.

TREVOR (*stunned*). I didn't know about any of this. There's no reference . . . are you sure that's what happened? My information is that William . . . (*He leafs through papers*) . . . wait a minute . . . here we are. 1938. Heart failure. And there's nothing about Edward . . . .

SISTER JULIAN. Ah well, Edward recovered very quickly. Never one of the casualties for long. I, on the other hand, was presumed to have suffered from some kind of nervous breakdown. It was the only way my behaviour could be explained. When I 'recovered', I was sent to a convalescent home run by nuns. Edward arranged it all. He paid the bills. He sent flowers and boxes of chocolates.

In the meantime, Charnwater was demolished. If you go there now you will see a neat, ugly little housing estate with privet hedges and sanitised plastic gardens sprayed with chemicals to keep anything nasty out. You'll find no trace of William's barley fields, and jungles and sand dunes. No ants, no butterflies, no cuckoopint, no harvest mice. Nothing like that.

TREVOR. That's another thing. There's no reference anywhere to all these paintings you say William did.

SISTER JULIAN. How could there be? No one knew. No one who might have valued them . . . no one who understood what an extraordinary thing he had done . . . ever saw them. William was mad. That's what the lawyers decided. Isn't it mad to try to gather everything that you love and fear will be lost under your roof? Isn't it mad to try to make something beautiful for no other reason except that?

TREVOR. *Were* the paintings of value?

SISTER JULIAN. What do you mean by 'value'?

TREVOR. You could have saved them.

SISTER JULIAN. On my own? (*Conceding.*) Yes, I could, Mr Norman. You're quite right. 'Charnwater is yours,' he said. 'Have it.' I should have insisted on that. I have no excuse. Such a weight of guilt. Think of it. I managed, indirectly, to kill the one and then, though I had the opportunity, I failed to kill the other. (*Shocked by what she's said.*) No, that's not right. That's not what I mean. But to be responsible for Edward still being alive and William not being . . . a world with Edward in it and no William . . . I couldn't live in a world like that. I couldn't stand it. So I ran away. As you can see. This was the one place in the world, I thought, where Edward couldn't finally get at me. The one place where I could live a simple, direct life . . . working in the garden, thinking . . . without the phone call or the telegram. No kind of blackmail could touch me here.

Of course he tried. He tried to get me out. And until I was

properly professed I was always afraid he might manage it. It was
an unusually long time, you see, before they let me take my vows.
They believed . . . quite rightly . . . that I had no real religious
vocation. They believed I was running away.

In those days they still cut off all our hair. It was part of the
final ceremony. One of the other novices wept but I suddenly
thought of the story Dora used to tell us about the princess who
was locked up in the tower. The prince climbed up her hair to
rescue her and I started laughing. Cut it all off, I thought, short
as you can.

(*Sadly.*) You see, if they'd been one man . . . that's what nature
intended. A perfect balance. But you can't have one without
the other.

'And the elder shall serve the younger.' That's how it ought to be.
Still, I've kept you too long, Mr Norman.

TREVOR. The problem is, Sister Julian . . . the rules of biography
. . . I will need to find corroborative evidence . . . letters . . .
diaries . . . anything you may still have.

SISTER JULIAN. The evidence is all around you. Everywhere you
look. You don't need anything else. This is a story, Mr Norman.
I told you from the beginning it was a story.

TREVOR. Yes but . . . .

SISTER JULIAN. You don't need corroborative evidence for that
kind of truth.

TREVOR. No.

SISTER JULIAN. Go away and write it.

The porteress will let you out. Remember . . . be very quiet until
you get outside the walls. Then make as much noise as you can.